Exploring

TECHNOLOGY

2

Biological Control–Cog Railroad

Marshall Cavendish
New York • London • Toronto • Sydney

Marshall Cavendish
99 White Plains Road
Tarrytown, New York 10591

www.marshallcavendish.com

© 2004 Marshall Cavendish Corporation

Created by **The Brown Reference Group plc**

Library of Congress Cataloging-in-Publication Data

Exploring technology.
　　p. cm.
　　Includes bibliographical references and index.
　　Contents: v. 1. ABR-BIC -- v. 2. BIO-COG -- v. 3. COL-END -- v. 4.
ENE-GEO -- v. 5. GLA-LEA -- v. 6. LIG-MOV -- v. 7. MUL-POT -- v. 8.
POW-SHI -- v. 9. SHI-TEL -- v. 10. TEL-WOO -- v. 11. Index.
　　ISBN 0-7614-7406-4 (set)
　　1. Technology--Encyclopedias.
　　T9 .E97 2003
　　603--dc21

　　　　　　　　　　　　　　　　　　　2002071510
　　ISBN 0-7614-7406-4 (set)
　　ISBN 0-7614-7408-0 (vol 2)

Printed in China.

08 07 06 05 04 03　5 4 3 2 1

PHOTOGRAPHIC CREDITS

Agricultural Research Service/USDA: Scott Bauer *84*; **Art Explosion:** *131t*; **Corbis:** Craig
Aumess *112*, Lester V Bergman *90t*, Bettmann *115*, Richard A Cooke *143*, Pablo Corral *157*,
Ecoscene/Chinch Gryniewicz *147, 154-155*, Eye Ubiquitous *123, 144*, Owen Franken *120*, Farrell
Grehan *111*, Gunter Marx Photography *102*, Wolfgang Kaehler *110*, Bob Krist *141*, Buddy Mays *106*;
The Purcell Team: *131b*, Roger Ressmeyer *153t*, Michael T Sedam *90b, 134-135*, Paul A Souders
119, Bob Witkowski *137*, Adam Woolfitt *122*; **Greyhound Lines:** *113*; **Hulton Archive:** *136*;
Image Bank: Jay Fries *88*, Romilly Lockyer *150*, Michael Melford *153b*, Juan Silva *98*, Andreas
Stirnberg *101*; **Life File:** Emma Lee *108*; **NASA:** Ames Research Center *129*, Johnson Space
Center *130*; **NHPA:** Michael Leach *85*; **PA Photos:** *86, 148*; **Pictor:** *91, 104, 117, 124-125, 127,
142, 146, 152*, Rick Brady *93*; **Science & Society Picture Library:** Science Museum *156*; **Stone:**
Ben Edwards *89*; **U.S. Dept of Defense:** Defense Visual Information Center *94, 133*

Front cover Corbis
Title page Digital Vision
Contents page Digital Vision

MARSHALL CAVENDISH

Project editor: Peter Mavrikis
Production manager: Alan Tsai
Editorial director: Paul Bernabeo

THE BROWN REFERENCE GROUP PLC

Project editor: Clive Carpenter
Deputy editor: Jim Martin
Design: Richard Berry, Alison Gardner
Picture research: Helen Simm, Susannah Jayes, Rebecca Cox
Illustrations: Darren Awuah, Dax Fullbrook, Mark Walker
Index: Kay Ollerenshaw
Managing editor: Bridget Giles

Exploring TECHNOLOGY

2

BIO-COG

Marshall Cavendish
New York • London • Toronto • Sydney

Biological Control

The use of living organisms to keep pest species in check

Every year, pests cause damage to millions of dollars worth of crops and farm animals. Finding ways to control pests is big business. Until recently, pest control has focused on using synthetic chemicals called pesticides to kill unwanted organisms. There is concern, however, about the effects of these chemicals on people's health and on the environment.

Today, natural methods of pest control are often used instead of pesticides. These methods involve the introduction of the pests' natural enemies to limit their numbers. This approach is called biological control.

The problem of introduction

Most pests have been introduced by people to the areas where they cause problems. Some introductions are accidental, such as that of European gypsy moths to North America. The caterpillars of these moths can munch through large patches of woodland. Some pest introductions have been deliberate. Water hyacinth was brought to the United States as an ornamental plant but soon began to clog major waterways.

In their native habitats, pest species do not cause problems because their numbers are kept in

HIGHLIGHTS

◆ Introducing a control agent does not usually eliminate a pest but keeps its numbers in check.

◆ Control organisms include predators and parasitoids, as well as organisms that compete with the pest.

◆ Biological control is strictly regulated today, following the damaging effects on the environment of some early programs.

check by natural enemies and other species that compete for food and space. In new habitats, these enemies are absent, and the populations of pests are able to explode.

Reaching a balance

Biologists may introduce a natural enemy into an area that is overrun by pests. Introducing natural enemies does not usually eliminate a pest, but instead their numbers reach a balance with the pest population.

There are two main types of natural enemies. Predators (PREH-duh-tuhrz) attack and feed on the pests. For example, ladybugs are beetles that feed on many other insects, especially aphids (A-fuhdz). Aphids are particularly damaging. Plants wither and die if too many aphids feed on their sap, and these pests also pass viruses from plant to plant. Ladybugs are often introduced around crops ravaged by aphids. They are good biological control organisms because both the adults and the young eat vast numbers of pests.

The second kind of natural enemy is called a parasitoid (PAR-uh-suh-TOID). Parasitoids are usually parasitic wasps or flies. Most parasitic wasps attack the eggs or young of insects, laying an egg inside. The egg hatches, and the wasp grub feeds on the internal organs of the pest. Eventually, the pest dies and the grub pupates (changes into an adult). Parasitoids are good

Introduced to Australia in 1935 to control cane beetles, cane toads are now major pests in their own right.

biological control organisms because many attack just one species of pest, and other nonpest insects are unaffected.

Other biological control agents

Many bacteria, viruses, and fungi are pathogens (agents that cause disease). Some are used to spread disease through pest populations. For example, *Bacillus thuringiensis* bacteria kill crop-eating caterpillars by releasing a toxic chemical when swallowed by the insect.

Occasionally, scientists introduce organisms to an affected area that do not feed on the pest. Instead, they compete with it for resources like food and space. These competitors are called antagonists. Most antagonists are microorganisms (very small life-forms) that prevent the growth of other, harmful types of microorganisms. For example, bacteria are sometimes used to protect wheat seeds. The seeds are coated with bacteria, which multiply quickly. The bacterial coating keeps fungi at bay.

Interfering with breeding

Some pests, such as certain flies, only mate once. This behavior can be exploited to control these pests. For example, before the early 1960s screwworms (larvae of a type of blowfly) caused enormous damage to cattle herds throughout the southern United States and Mexico. These larvae burrow into flesh to grow. To control the screwworms, scientists reared large numbers of male adult flies. The scientists sterilized them (made them unable to breed) using radiation before releasing them. The sterilized flies mated with wild females, but since they were sterile the females could not lay fertile eggs. This program was extremely successful, and by 1991 these damaging pests had been completely eliminated from the United States and Mexico.

Programs like this demonstrate that scientists working on a biological control program must have an intimate knowledge of the biology of the species involved.

In control

Biological control is subject to stringent testing procedures. Before scientists release new control organisms into the wild, they must be certain that the organism targets only the pest, and that nonpest species are unharmed.

CHECK THESE OUT!
✔CROP FARMING ✔HORTICULTURE
✔LIVESTOCK FARMING ✔PESTICIDE AND HERBICIDE

LOOK CLOSER

Out of control

Although biological control programs today are closely scrutinized by scientists, many earlier introductions were not tested rigorously enough and caused great damage to the environment. For example, cane toads were introduced to Australia from South America in 1935. These toads were intended to kill the cane beetles that at the time were devastating plantations. In addition to eating the beetles, however, the toads began to feed on a wide range of native nonpest insects and small amphibians. Cane toads are also poisonous, and predators that fed on the toads died. These toads remain a serious problem throughout Australia.

In 1978, another disastrous introduction was carried out. Predatory *Euglandina* snails were released on a number of South Pacific islands to control giant African land snails. Rather than attacking these large snails, *Euglandina* instead attacked the native *Partula* snails. Within ten years, every species of wild native snail on islands such as Moorea and Tahiti had been wiped out. Just a few native species survive in zoos and research centers.

Bionics

Artificial replacement of parts of the human body

Human bodies are remarkable pieces of natural engineering, but they do not last forever. Some people lose parts of their body through accidents, illness, or wear. Others are born with an arm or a leg missing. Scientists have developed a range of artificial devices to replace parts of the body that are damaged or absent. Using engineering techniques to replace body parts is called bionics, or biomedical engineering.

HIGHLIGHTS

◆ Replacement joints are made from tough, long-lasting materials to survive wear and tear inside the human body.

◆ Each artificial limb is carefully molded to fit the person who will wear it.

◆ Electrical implants can help deaf people hear; one day they may help blind people see, too.

U.S. athlete Marlon Ray Shirley won silver in the high jump in the 2000 Sydney Paralympic Games.

Replacement joints

The human skeleton serves as an efficient machine. It includes a collection of levers that can turn small forces into much larger ones. For example, arms work like miniature crowbars, so a small movement at the elbow becomes a much larger movement at the wrist.

Movements put tremendous pressure on joints such as the elbow, wrist, knee, and hip. People make a huge number of movements during their lifetime. A person may make more than a million walking movements every year. The forces exerted during these movements can gradually wear out joints such as the hips.

Replacement joints are made from advanced metals, plastics, and ceramics. Sometimes, several different materials are used together in one joint. For example, an artificial hip joint is a metal ball that moves smoothly in a polyethylene (pah-LEE-ETH-uh-leen; plastic) socket.

The socket itself is fixed inside a larger metal socket. Both ends of the artificial joint are firmly attached to the patient's bones.

Artificial limbs

Sometimes people lose their limbs, or have to have them amputated (cut off) because of accidents or illnesses. In some countries, people lose limbs by stepping on land mines left behind after wars have ended. Artificial legs were once little more than stumps of wood. Today, much more advanced prostheses (prahs-THEE-ses), or artificial limbs, are available. Modern prostheses contain weights, springs, and levers. These replacements allow amputees (people who have lost limbs) to walk and pick objects up and hold them. The end of an artificial limb is molded to attach comfortably to the remainder of the person's limb. Artificial limbs are made of plastic that looks just like real ones.

When amputees lose a limb, they also lose the muscles that move it and the nerves that control it. To compensate for the lack of muscles, weights and springs are used to swing an artificial leg naturally into position. Artificial arms are much the same. A person who has lost one arm may have to use their good arm to move the artificial one into position. Some artificial arms are battery powered, with electronic controls to open and close the fingers at the touch of a switch. Artificial legs cannot be made in this way yet because portable batteries are not powerful enough to drive the leg for long.

Electrical implants

Sometimes, people are unable to use or control limbs or organs. This is caused by a problem with the body's nervous system (the network that connects the body to the brain). Bionic engineers solve this problem with electrical implants. These electrical devices amplify (increase in strength) the body's nervous signals if they are too weak, or send out entirely new signals if the body or brain are not sending out signals of their own.

A heart pacemaker is an electrical implant. This tiny, battery-powered device sends trigger signals when needed to a person's heart to keep it beating regularly. Another common implant is the electrical cochlear (KO-klee-uhr) implant, a device that helps deaf people hear. It includes a tiny microphone that is placed outside the ear. The microphone is wired to a speaker that is surgically implanted next to the cochlea, a sensitive part of the inner ear. The cochlea converts incoming sounds into electrical signals that the brain can understand. Cochlear implants can greatly improve hearing in many deaf people.

Bionic engineers hope they will one day be able to do something similar for blind people, using miniature video cameras to send signals directly to the visual cortex (the part of the brain that interprets information from the eyes).

CHECK THESE OUT!
✔HEART-LUNG MACHINE ✔MECHANICS
✔MEDICAL TECHNOLOGY ✔ROBOTICS

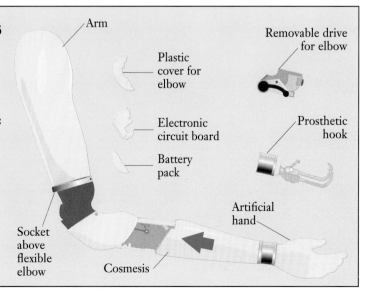

LOOK CLOSER

Artificial arms

This artificial arm (right) uses electrical signals from the remnant of the patient's arm to control the replacement elbow, wrist, and hand. To give a realistic appearance, almost the entire mechanism is covered by a skinlike layer called a cosmesis (kuhz-MEE-ses).

An artificial hand can be a cosmetic casting that does not move. Today, surgeons fit many amputees with artificial hands that are electronically controlled devices that allow the patient to pick things up and hold them. When necessary, an artificial hand can be replaced with a prosthetic hook.

Arm

Plastic cover for elbow

Electronic circuit board

Battery pack

Removable drive for elbow

Prosthetic hook

Artificial hand

Socket above flexible elbow

Cosmesis

Biotechnology

Using organisms to make useful substances

Computers and cars changed the lives of people who lived in the 20th century. Biotechnology may change lives just as drastically in the 21st century. Biotechnologists use their understanding of how living cells and the chemicals inside them work to make things that are useful. Some biotechnologists use organisms to manufacture substances like medicines and other chemicals. Others copy the way organisms make these substances in nature.

Tiny workers

Although biotechnology is a new field, people who make cheese, beer, and wine have used organisms for thousands of years. Brewers use microorganisms called yeast to turn sugars into alcohol in beer. Microorganisms are widely used in biotechnology. Animals and plants are made up of millions of individual units called cells, but many microorganisms are made of just one cell. Perhaps the best-known microorganisms are bacteria. Bacteria live almost everywhere, from high in the air to deep beneath the surface of the Earth. Some infect cuts or cause upset stomachs. Bacteria also cause devastating diseases. Both anthrax and plague are caused by bacteria.

HIGHLIGHTS

♦ Microorganisms, such as bacteria, are grown inside tanks called bioreactors.

♦ Enzymes are important biotechnological tools, used to produce complex chemicals.

♦ The makers of products such as beer, wine, yogurt, and cheese use biotechnology.

Bacteria and other single-celled organisms, such as yeast, amoebas, and algae, multiply very quickly through a process called binary fission: they simply divide into two. Biotechnologists take advantage of this division of cells to make large amounts of substances quickly.

Inside the cell

Single-celled organisms and the cells in the bodies of larger organisms have several things in common. Each cell is surrounded by a thin layer called the cell membrane. Within the membrane, the cell contains DNA (deoxyribonucleic acid),

Technicians working in laboratories and biotechnological factories wear protective clothing including plastic overalls, hats, gloves, and special footwear. These items of clothing guard against contact with the contents of tank bioreactors. Any such contact could introduce contamination to the finished product.

a long chain of chemicals joined in a twisted ladder shape. The DNA chain holds the instructions, called genes, for making new cells. Many non-bacterial cells keep their DNA within another membrane called the cell nucleus. Genetic engineering, a major field of biotechnology, changes a cell's DNA to alter the output of a cell. The rest of the cell consists of cytoplasm (SY-tuh-plaz-uhm), a gel-like liquid where the cell's life processes take place. Plant cells are a little different. They have an extra cell wall around them made of cellulose, a chemical that contains chains of sugar molecules.

Bioreactors

Biotechnology uses machines called bioreactors to grow microorganisms and other cells on a large scale. The vats used to make beer were among the first bioreactors, and modern versions are very similar. The most common type of bioreactor is called a tank bioreactor. This is a large steel vat that holds a mixture, called a broth, of microorganisms and the nutrients (nourishment) they need to survive. Before the broth is added to the tank, the equipment is sterilized to kill unwanted microorganisms that might be lurking inside the tank. Rogue microorganisms in the bioreactor could damage the final products and can make them poisonous. Once inside the tank, the broth is kept in the best condition for fast growth. A computer controls the temperature, oxygen level, and pH (the degree of acidity) inside the tank. Oxygen is bubbled through the tank when necessary, and stirrers keep the broth well mixed.

Tank bioreactors grow microorganisms, usually bacteria. These organisms must be tough to thrive inside the large, swirling tank. The largest bioreactors can hold 265,000 gallons (1 million liters) of broth. Tank bioreactor organisms make some very important chemicals, like insulin. Insulin is a type of hormone (chemical messenger) made in the pancreas. It controls the amount of sugar in a person's blood. Bioengineered insulin is given to diabetic people, who cannot make the hormone themselves.

The hormone is grown in a bioreactor by *Escherichia coli* (usually called *E. coli*) bacteria that have had the gene for human insulin inserted

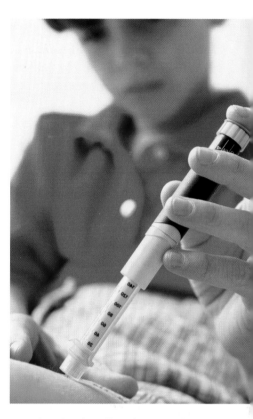

Diabetic people need to inject insulin. This is often made using bioengineered bacteria.

into their DNA. Before this advance, people with diabetes had to inject insulin taken from a pig or cow, but insulin from other mammals does not work well in people.

Making cells

Some types of bioreactors grow individual cells of animals, plants, and other multicellular (many-celled) organisms. The cells of these organisms are fragile compared to bacteria, and they would quickly be damaged inside a tank reactor. Instead, scientists grow these cells in conditions that are similar to those inside an organism's body. The delicate cells are held in a mesh and are surrounded by an artificial membrane, similar to the one that coats each cell. The mesh is bathed in a liquid containing the nutrients that the cells need, and no stirring is required. Although bioreactors like this cannot produce cells as quickly as large tank bioreactors, they can make large amounts of substances such as antibodies, which are an essential part of an animal's immune (self-defense) system.

The cells are separated from the rest of the broth and extracted in a number of different ways. Filters may be used to remove the solid cells from the liquid. Sometimes, the cells are separated by adding chemicals that make the cells clump together. The clumps gradually sink to the bottom of the tank. Cells can also be separated out by using a centrifuge (SEN-truh-fyooj). This machine spins the broth quickly so the heavier cells settle out.

Scientists use **E. coli** *bacteria to produce insulin. The gene for insulin is inserted into the bacteria, and the bacteria multiply inside a bioreactor.*

Using biotechnology

Many industries make products using microorganisms. The food industry has used microorganisms for many centuries. Biotechnology is also used to produce new foods. Scientists alter plants, introducing genes to make crops that grow faster and larger than natural varieties. Changing plants and animals by introducing genes is called genetic engineering.

Biotechnology has also changed medicine. For many years, molds have been grown to produce antibiotics (drugs that kill or stop disease-causing

bacteria). Biotechnologists also produce reagents (substances that cause reactions) that can test whether a donated organ can be transplanted into a sick person.

Some people worry that introducing new genes to plants and animals might cause dramatic environmental problems or help new diseases become established. Yet microorganisms can be beneficial to the environment. Some microorganisms are used to help clean up spilled oil and other pollution and to break down sewage. These treatments yield gases that can be used for fuel—a valuable renewable energy resource.

Perhaps the most exciting products of biotechnology are biosensors. These are devices that combine a biological substance, such as an enzyme, with electronics to detect chemicals in their surroundings. One day, biosensors might be used inside our bodies as parts of tiny micromachines, designed to warn us if we are becoming ill. These machines might also be able to supply medicines and help send them to places where they are needed.

CHECK THESE OUT!
✔BIONICS ✔BREWING INDUSTRY ✔CENTRIFUGE
✔CHEMICAL ENGINEERING ✔GENETIC ENGINEERING

LOOK CLOSER

Enzymes

Enzymes are substances that speed up reactions inside cells and elsewhere in an organism's body. Without enzymes, biological reactions would only happen very slowly or not at all. Enzymes are vital—they are involved in just about every life process, from breaking down food in the stomach to copying DNA when a cell divides. All enzymes are proteins (chains of smaller chemicals called amino acids).

None of the processes used in biotechnology would be possible without enzymes. For example, it is the enzymes in yeast that turn sugar into alcohol to make beer. Enzymes are used to cut up and reassemble strands of DNA exactly. Biological detergents contain enzymes that break down dirt in clothing. Each type of enzyme has its own unique shape—it is the shape of an enzyme that lets it do its job. The substances that react during a chemical change join onto the enzyme at a point called the active site. This action alters the enzyme's shape, pushing the substances together. When the substances come together they react and produce a new chemical or set of chemicals. If enzymes get too hot, their structure breaks down. However, scientists have extracted enzymes that are effective at high temperatures from bacteria that live in hot springs.

This hot spring's colors are produced by bacteria, some of which are used in biotechnology.

Blast Furnace

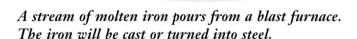

A vessel used to make iron and other metals

The blast furnace is named for the blast of hot air that it uses to heat iron ore (rock that contains lots of iron), allowing pure metal to be extracted. Modern furnaces were developed around 350 years ago. With the iron they produced, engineers built bridges, steam engines, industrial machines, and railroads. This new technology drove the 18th-century Industrial Revolution, which helped shape the modern world. Other metals, such as copper, can also be extracted from their ores in blast furnaces.

A stream of molten iron pours from a blast furnace. The iron will be cast or turned into steel.

Making iron

There are several types of iron ores. Most consist of iron oxides (iron combined with oxygen) mixed with other minerals such as silica. The main ores mined for producing iron are hematite (HEE-muh-TYT) and magnetite (MAG-nuh-tyt), which contain 50 to 70 percent iron oxide.

The ironmaking process smelts (extracts) iron from its ore by heating it with other materials that react strongly with oxygen. These materials remove oxygen from the iron oxides in the ores. The most suitable material to use in smelting is carbon, which is easily obtained from coal. The carbon burns to form carbon dioxide gas. This gas reacts with more of the carbon to become carbon monoxide gas. The carbon monoxide then removes the oxygen from the iron oxides, reducing them to iron.

Early ironmakers heated iron ore with carbon in the form of charcoal. Charcoal was burned to produce carbon dioxide and carbon monoxide. The carbon monoxide combined with the oxygen in the ore and carried it away, leaving the iron.

Temperatures in these early furnaces were high enough to make iron but were not sufficient to melt the metal completely. The iron produced was spongy and brittle. It contained impurities such as silica, but it could be hardened by repeated hammering. The blast of hot air into a blast furnace allows smelting to take place at higher temperatures, which allows more carbon to be absorbed and the iron to melt completely. Molten metal can be poured into molds to make strong cast-iron objects, or converted into steel.

Inside the blast furnace

Modern blast furnaces are huge. They can be as much as 200 feet (60 m) high. The main vessel of the furnace can be around 100 feet (30 m) tall and 25 feet (8 m) in diameter, with a lining of heat-resistant material more than 3 feet (1 m) thick. This lining is designed to withstand high temperatures inside the furnace. The largest blast furnaces can produce up to 13,000 tons (11,800 metric tons) of iron each day.

A blast furnace keeps working nonstop, apart from maintenance breaks, until the lining wears out—this can take ten years or more. Iron ore is

---

HIGHLIGHTS

♦ Nearly all the world's iron is produced in blast furnaces.

♦ Blast furnaces can reach 200 feet (60 m) high.

♦ Some modern blast furnaces produce up to 13,000 tons (11,800 metric tons) of iron per day.

loaded into the top of the furnace, along with coke (a carbon-rich material) and crushed limestone. At the bottom of the furnace, hot air at a temperature of up to 1600°F (870°C) blasts in through pipes called tuyeres (twee-YERZ). When coke meets the hot air, it reacts with the oxygen in the air and burns to form carbon dioxide. This reaction also releases a lot of heat, and the temperature at the bottom of the furnace rises to around 3600°F (2000°C). The hot carbon dioxide rises through the furnace, reacting with more coke to form carbon monoxide. The carbon monoxide combines with the oxygen that is in the ore and reduces the iron oxide to iron.

Collecting the iron

Molten iron trickles down to the base of the furnace. At the same time, the limestone melts and fuses with silica and other impurities in the

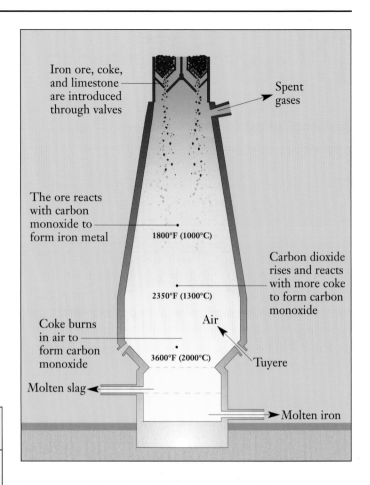

Iron ore, coke, and limestone are introduced through valves

Spent gases

The ore reacts with carbon monoxide to form iron metal

1800°F (1000°C)

Carbon dioxide rises and reacts with more coke to form carbon monoxide

2350°F (1300°C)

Air

Coke burns in air to form carbon monoxide

3600°F (2000°C)

Tuyere

Molten slag

Molten iron

A cross section view of a typical blast furnace.

iron to become a waste product called slag. The molten iron collects at the base of the furnace with the slag floating on top. When enough iron has collected, a plug in the side of the furnace base is opened. The iron and slag run out and flow along a trench, from where the slag is diverted into ladles or pits. The iron is poured into cylindrical, heatproof railroad cars and taken to another part of the plant to be made into steel or cast into ingots (bars in a convenient shape for storage). The slag is processed to make construction materials such as concrete, road fill, and railroad ballast.

At the top of the furnace, the hot gases are carried away by large pipes. The gases are cooled and the dust they carry is removed. Most of the waste gas is carbon monoxide that has not reacted with oxygen in the iron ore. This gas is burned to heat the brick-lined stoves that produce the hot-air blast.

HISTORY

The history of blast furnaces

c. 500 B.C.E. The Chinese discover the principle of the blast furnace.

1500 C.E. The first European blast furnace is built at Liège, Belgium.

1621 At the town of Dudley, England, Dud Dudley builds the first blast furnace to be heated by coal instead of charcoal.

1644 John Winthrop, Jr. builds the first blast furnace for iron making in North America at what is now West Quincy, Massachusetts.

1709 English ironmaker Abraham Darby mass-produces iron using coke instead of coal.

1712 Abraham Darby makes the iron cylinders for the world's first steam engine, built by English engineer Thomas Newcomen.

1824 Scottish ironmaker James B. Neilson invents the first system for preheating the blast air.

CHECK THESE OUT!
✔CASTING ✔IRON AND STEEL ✔METALS

Blood Transfusion

The transfer of blood from one person to another

On average, a person's body contains about ten pints (4.7 liters) of blood. Blood is composed of a watery liquid called plasma, with red blood cells that carry oxygen and white blood cells that guard against infection. Blood also contains cell fragments called platelets, which form scabs over damaged tissue. It carries many chemicals, such as hormones (messenger chemicals), around the body, as well as waste products such as carbon dioxide.

Blood loss

People can lose a lot of blood during operations, or after an accident. This blood needs to be replaced quickly. Doctors replace it with blood provided by a person called the donor. The process of replacement is called transfusion.

Blood can be transfused "whole," to save the lives of people who have lost a lot of blood in an accident or operation. Sometimes, just one part of blood, such as plasma, is given to patients suffering from a particular illness. The earliest human blood transfusions were carried out during the early 19th century. In 1900, Austrian scientist Karl Landsteiner (1868–1943) made a key discovery that improved transfusions. He found

HIGHLIGHTS

◆ Blood transfusions involve the transfer of blood from one person to another.

◆ Blood transfusions became widespread after 1900, when scientists discovered that people have different blood groups.

◆ Patients may receive whole blood or just one of its constituents, such as plasma.

that some people's blood made the blood cells of others clump together. These clumps could block blood vessels if they entered a patient's bloodstream during a transfusion, causing death. The discovery led to the identification of different blood types, later called A, B, and O. Giving the wrong type of blood to patients could be avoided by identifying their blood group beforehand.

Giving blood

Blood donors help save lives. People give blood either at a hospital or at a temporary medical center. About a pint of blood (470 ml) is taken from a vein in the donor's arm. The collected blood undergoes tests to check for diseases. If it is fit for use, the blood is stored in airtight bags and refrigerated. During a transfusion, blood may simply flow into the patient, or it may be pumped in. Recently, artificial blood has been developed. In the future, the use of artificial blood will reduce the risk of infection during transfusion. Artificial blood developed to date cannot perform many of the functions performed by real blood.

CHECK THESE OUT!
✔CENTRIFUGE ✔HEART-LUNG MACHINE
✔MEDICAL TECHNOLOGY ✔SURGERY

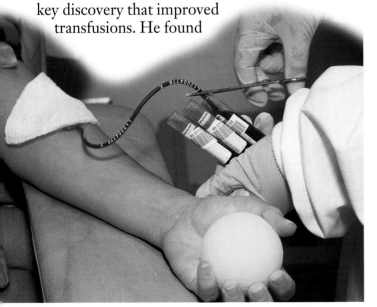

A doctor inserts a needle into a vein. The donor squeezes a soft ball while blood is drawn.

Bomb and Shell

Explosive devices used in warfare

Since the discovery of gunpowder by Chinese scientists around 850 C.E. and its spread to Europe around 1,000 years ago, military engineers have invented many weapons that utilize its destructive power. Discoveries of other explosives, such as TNT (trinitrotoluene; tri-ni-tro-TUHL-ya-wen), accelerated the development of these weapons, which include bombs, shells, and grenades.

HIGHLIGHTS

- ◆ Bombs are explosive devices that must be delivered to their targets.

- ◆ Shells are explosive devices fired from artillery.

- ◆ Grenades are small explosive devices thrown by hand or launched from guns.

Delivering bombs

There are many different types of bombs. Terrorists use bombs that consist of explosives set off by timers or trigger switches. Military bombs are often dropped from aircraft to damage targets and kill people on the ground. Most military bombs carry fuses set to make them explode when they hit the target, but some are designed to explode in the air just above the target. Others bury themselves in the ground before exploding to destroy underground targets.

Military bombs were first used in southeast Europe, in the First Balkan War (1912–1913), when pilots dropped homemade explosive packages from aircraft by hand. The first aircraft built to carry and drop bombs went into action during World War I (1914–1918), and aircraft dropped millions of tons of bombs onto ground targets during World War II (1939–1945).

Until the middle of World War II, aircraft crews had no control over bombs after they had dropped them. The crews could not guide the bombs directly onto their targets. In 1942, scientists invented radio-controlled bombs. Using radio signals, crews could adjust wings and fins on the bombs to steer them. By 1945, some bombs also carried television cameras. These cameras enabled the crew to see the targets and steer the bombs directly toward them. Modern versions of these bombs, called smart bombs, are guided by laser beams. A projector on the aircraft shines a laser beam onto the target. The bomb detects laser light reflected from the target, then steers toward it.

However, not all bombs deliver explosives. Incendiary (fire) bombs are packed with materials that are designed to burn fiercely and set fire to buildings.

Firing shells

A shell is a bomb fired from artillery (weapons, such as cannons, that fire missiles). Shells contain explosives or other harmful materials and use fuses to make them explode on impact or just before they hit the target. The

Artillery is used to launch shells at enemy positions.

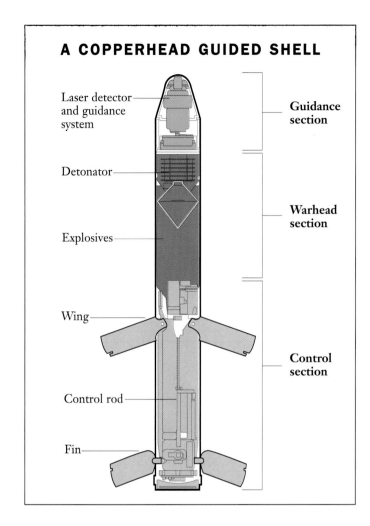

A COPPERHEAD GUIDED SHELL

Laser detector and guidance system — Guidance section

Detonator —

Explosives — Warhead section

Wing —

Control section

Control rod —

Fin —

smoke shells burst in midair and release a number of canisters. These canisters spread along the ground producing a smoke screen.

Most shells are unguided. Once they leave the gun, the gunner has no control over them and cannot be certain that they will hit the target. Guided shells are much more accurate. Like smart bombs, they home in on laser beams reflected from the target. They are steered with wings and fins that flip out from their casings when they leave the gun barrel.

Throwing grenades

A grenade is a small bomb that soldiers throw at enemy troops, vehicles, and buildings. To make them safe to use, most grenades have a simple timing device. There is a spring-loaded lever on the side of the grenade, held in place by a locking pin. The thrower holds the lever tightly, removes the pin, and throws the grenade at the target. As soon as the grenade leaves the thrower's hand, the lever springs out and starts the timing device. The grenade explodes a few seconds later.

Soldiers can throw hand grenades 130 feet (40 m) or more. To reach more distant targets, they use grenade launchers fitted to rifles. The grenades can be fired up to 1,300 feet (400 m). These grenades do not have lever-operated timers, but they explode on impact instead.

CHECK THESE OUT!
✔MISSILE ✔TORPEDO AND DEPTH CHARGE

blast damages buildings and kills or injures people. Shell fragments, or shrapnel, also kill and maim. Some specialized shells can blast through thick steel armor. These shells have a pointed nose made of hardened steel. The point can penetrate the armor of a warship or a tank.

When a HEAT (high explosive antitank) shell explodes, it creates a narrow, high-speed blast of hot gas and molten metal. The blast can pierce armor up to 3 feet (1 m) thick. HEP (high explosive plastic) antitank shells have thin metal casings filled with plastic explosives. When a HEP shell hits a tank, the casing splits open. The plastic explosive sticks to the target before it explodes, blasting a large chunk of armor into the inside of the tank.

Shells are also used to create smoke to hide troop movements. A small explosive charge bursts open a shell containing white phosphorus (FAHS-fuh-ruhs). The phosphorus burns, releasing a cloud of dense white smoke. Some

PEOPLE

Henry Shrapnel

Henry Shrapnel (1761–1842) was an English army officer who invented a new type of shell. This small, rounded iron shell contained lead shot and an explosive that was set off by a timing fuse. The fuse was timed to explode the shell when it was in the air above the heads of enemy troops. The exploding shell created a hail of lead shot that caused terrible injuries. Shrapnel is still a much-feared weapon. Rather than using lead shot, modern shrapnel shells cause damage when high-explosives burst the shell casing into many small jagged fragments.

Brake Systems

Systems to slow or stop moving vehicles or machines

Cars and most other machines with moving parts need brakes to help them stop. Brake systems apply force to the moving parts to slow or stop them. On a bicycle, for example, pulling on the brake lever creates the braking force. The lever pulls the brake cable, which draws the brake blocks against the rim of the wheel, slowing it down. The brake system transfers the force from the cyclist's hand to the moving wheel. The wheel is slowed due to friction—the rubbing between the brake blocks and the rim. Friction creates heat, and the brake blocks, or shoes, can become very hot. On a bicycle brake, the surrounding air soon cools the shoes, and heat is not a problem. If brakes on motorized vehicles overheat, they become much less effective.

Types of brakes

In early brakes, such as those on stagecoaches, a lever forced a block of wood or rubber against the rim of a moving wheel. These are called block brakes, and the bicycle brake is a modern example. Disk brake systems work like bicycle brakes, but they squeeze the brake blocks (called brake pads) against a disk attached to the wheel instead of against the wheel rim. Some cars, motorcycles, and airplane wheels have disk brakes. Drum brakes are brake blocks that work

HIGHLIGHTS

◆ Bicycles have block brakes operated by cables.

◆ Cars have disk brakes and drum brakes operated by hydraulic systems.

◆ Large trucks have drum brakes operated by compressed air systems.

◆ Aircraft have rows of disk brakes operated by hydraulic systems.

from the inside. A pair of brake blocks (called brake shoes) press outward against the inside rim of a steel drum attached to the wheel. Cars, motorcycles, and most trucks have drum brakes.

Road vehicle brakes

Early cars had drum brakes on each wheel. But by 1940, most cars used hydraulic (hy-DRAW-lik) brake systems. Pressing the brake pedal forces a type of oil through a system of pipes. Force transferred through the fluid operates a series of pistons (sliding disks that fit inside cylinders) that drive the braking system. When

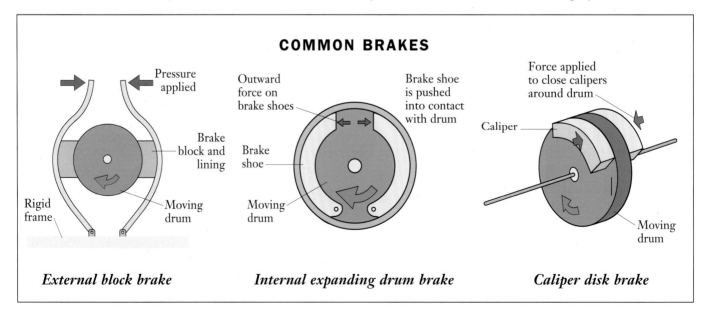

COMMON BRAKES

Pressure applied

Brake block and lining

Rigid frame

Moving drum

External block brake

Outward force on brake shoes

Brake shoe is pushed into contact with drum

Brake shoe

Moving drum

Internal expanding drum brake

Force applied to close calipers around drum

Caliper

Moving drum

Caliper disk brake

Four-wheel Hydraulic Brake Systems

LOOK CLOSER

Not all automobiles have four-wheel drive systems in which power is provided to all of the wheels. But four-wheel hydraulic braking systems are standard. In these systems, disk brakes stop the front wheels and drum brakes stop the rear wheels.

Pressure on the brake pedals is transmitted along a bar called the push rod. The push rod transmits pressure into the power-assist unit, where part of the engine's power is used to multiply the force that is applied by the driver. The power-assist unit, in turn, exerts pressure on the master cylinder, which has two pistons that force oil into the front and rear hydraulic lines. The hydraulic lines link the master cylinder with each of the four brakes. A valve called the combination valve regulates oil flow. It triggers an indicator on the dashboard if the pressure in either line drops because of a leak.

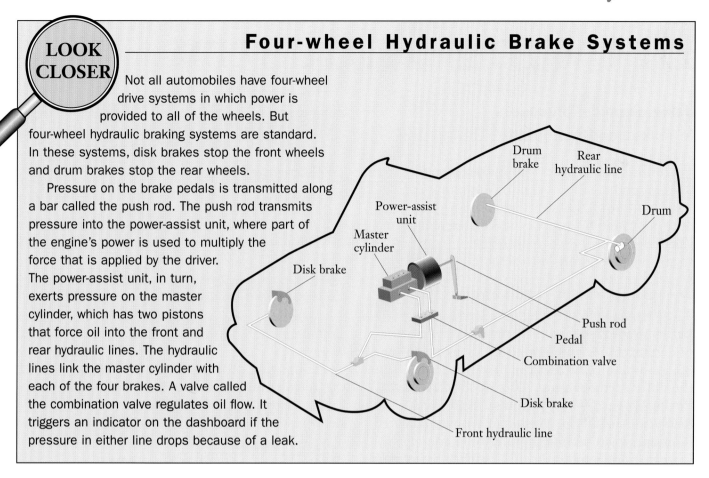

Drum brake
Rear hydraulic line
Power-assist unit
Master cylinder
Drum
Disk brake
Push rod
Pedal
Combination valve
Disk brake
Front hydraulic line

the driver releases the brake pedal, springs push the pistons back to release the brakes. Brake pads are made of synthetic fibers and ceramics.

To make brakes more powerful, many cars have power assist. When a driver pushes on the brake pedal, suction from the engine increases the pressure in the hydraulic system. This increases the force on the brake pistons in turn. Cars also have parking brakes to stop them from rolling away when they are parked. A parking brake is operated by a lever, which is connected by cable to the car's rear brakes. When the lever is pulled, the rear brakes are held on.

Because they are heavy, trucks need a greater braking force than cars. To provide extra force, truck brakes use compressed (squeezed) air from a compressor driven by the engine. Compressed air either adds pressure to hydraulic brakes, or works brake pistons directly. The brake pedal controls the air pressure and the amount of force.

Some road vehicles have antilock braking systems (ABS) that use electronic sensors to monitor wheel speed. If one wheel slows too fast, the car may skid and possibly crash. The ABS

computer detects this and releases and reapplies pressure on the locked wheel at 10-15 pulses each second. The wheel slows but does not skid.

Aircraft brakes

Aircraft also need powerful brakes to stop them when they land, but brakes alone cannot bring a large airplane to a halt. When a large jet touches down, deflectors at the rear of each engine swing into place to direct the thrust of the engines forward, slowing the plane down. At the same time, flaps on the upper surface of the wings flip up to act as air brakes. The wheel brakes are only applied after the reverse thrust and air brakes have slowed the plane. If they are applied too soon, they will overheat and could catch fire.

Airplane wheel brakes are disk brakes, with disks made of lightweight carbon fibers. There are usually a number of disks next to each other on a single shaft, with brake pads between them. This helps generate a very large braking force.

CHECK THESE OUT!
✔AIRCRAFT DESIGN ✔AUTOMOBILE ✔BICYCLE

Brewing Industry

Using chemical processes to make beer from grain

Brewing, the process that makes beer, is thought to have begun in Mesopotamia (modern Iraq) 8,000 years ago. The alcohol in beer is formed by a process called fermentation. Tiny organisms called yeast ferment (convert) sugar in cereal grains into alcohol.

Steeping, starch, and sugars

The first stage in brewing is called steeping. Barley grain is soaked in water at a temperature of 55°F to 60°F (13°C to 16°C). Soaking softens the grain and removes unwanted impurities from the outer seed covering. After about three days, the barley germinates (sprouts). Traditional breweries spread the steeped grain over a heated floor and sprinkle it with water to encourage germination. Modern breweries place the barley into a rotating drum. Warm, moist air then blows through the drum to speed up germination.

During germination, biological catalysts (substances that speed up chemical reactions) become active inside the grains. These catalysts, called enzymes (EN-zims), begin to break down the starches into sugars. Sugars are needed later

Mash tuns in a modern brewery. The quality of water used in mashing can affect the taste.

in the brewing process, so the brewer packs the germinating grain into a drying kiln to stop further growth. If germination continued, the sugar reserves of the barley would be depleted.

Malting and mashing

Temperatures in the kiln vary from 120°F (49°C) to 225°F (107°C). Temperature affects the flavor, color, and other qualities of the beer. Huge machines called threshers separate dried grain, or malt, from its seed covering. Crushing machines pound the malt into powder. Powdered malt and water are mashed in a huge vat called a mash tun, or cooker. Many breweries add other products, such as molasses (unrefined sugar) or extra enzymes. Mash is then heated. Temperatures in the tun vary from brewery to brewery, between around 120°F (49°C) to 170°F (77°C). Varying levels of heat cause more or less of the remaining starch to break down into a sugar called maltose (MOL-toz). Maltose also affects the taste of the beer. After several hours, solid particles in the mash are filtered out, leaving a liquid called wort.

Fermentation

Before fermentation takes place, dried hops (the fruit of a type of vine) may be added to the wort. Heat and pressure release oils from hops, which add a distinctive bitter flavor to the brew. After about two hours, filters sift out the remains of the hops, and the wort is set aside to cool.

THE BREWING PROCESS

Barley arrives from a granary.

Steeping and germination release sugars from the barley grain.

The barley grain is dried to prevent sprouting. Sugars produced during germination are retained.

Mashing heats the malt with water, releasing sugars from the malt and creating wort.

— Mash tun

Hops or other flavorings are mixed with the wort and sterilized by boiling for two hours.

Yeast is added to the wort and converts sugars to alcohol by fermentation, producing green beer.

The green beer is conditioned in large casks or tanks.

The finished beer is bottled for sale.

Most breweries use similar techniques, but different ingredients and temperatures are used.

Breweries guard details of the fermentation process to protect their unique products from competitors. They use a fungus called brewer's yeast to ferment sugars in wort. Some breweries have developed their own strains. Fermenting sugars yield ethanol (which forms the alcohol in beer) and carbon dioxide. All breweries follow either a top or bottom fermentation process.

Lager is a pale, fizzy beer. It is bottom-fermented, with the yeast growing at the depths of the cool wort. Bottom fermentation takes place at temperatures from 39°F to 54°F (4°C to 12°C). Darker beers, such as English bitter, are top-fermented. Carbon dioxide is bubbled through the brew, lifting the yeasts to the top of the vat. Top fermentation takes place at between 58°F and 68°F (14°C and 20°C).

The finished product

Bottom fermentation takes between five and 14 days to complete. Top fermentation takes two to five days. In both cases, the resulting liquid, called green beer, is filtered into sealed tanks. Conditioning and extra fermentation remove waste material, as well as forcing carbon dioxide through the liquid. This gas gives beer its fizz. Finally, beer is heated to 140°F (60°C) to kill off any remaining yeast or harmful bacteria.

CHECK THESE OUT!
✔BEVERAGES ✔BIOTECHNOLOGY
✔FOOD PRESERVATION ✔FOOD TECHNOLOGY

LOOK CLOSER

Ice beer

Ice brewing is a way of making and conditioning lager in very cold temperatures. German immigrants brought the technique to the United States in the 1840s. In the original method, beer ferments for a long time at temperatures close to freezing. The beer is then stored in barrels that are kept in very cold conditions. Over time, the beer develops an especially crisp and clean-tasting flavor. Ice beer has enjoyed a recent revival. The well-known breweries of Milwaukee and St. Louis, such as Miller, Pabst, and Anheuser-Busch, now specialize in producing their own versions of ice beer using original methods.

Brick and Masonry

Long-lasting building materials made from clay or cut stone

The first bricks, made around 10,000 years ago in southwest Asia, were very different from those used today. These bricks were made from mud and straw, shaped by hand, and then dried in the sun. They were rounded instead of rectangular and looked like large loaves of bread.

Rectangular bricks appeared 9,000 years ago in the eastern Mediterranean, when people began to use wooden boxes as molds. These bricks were all the same shape, so they were better for building. Later bricks were made from clay and fired (baked) in hot ovens called kilns. The Romans used bricks extensively. After the fall of the Roman Empire in the 5th century C.E., brick building declined until the 14th century.

Brick making

Most bricks are made of clay. This naturally occurring mineral is based on compounds of aluminum, silicon, and oxygen. Particles of clay readily stick together in clumps and soak up a great deal of water. When it is wet, clay is extremely plastic (flexible), and it can be molded into virtually any shape. Firing clay in a kiln

at temperatures of around 1800°F (1000°C) permanently changes its physical properties. The clay particles join together in a mass that remains hard even when it cools down. Different types of bricks are made from different clays, sometimes with other materials added to give them different properties and colors. Although bricks may sometimes look less attractive than stone, they cost less and often last longer.

Bricklaying

The process of putting bricks together to make walls and bigger structures is called bricklaying. This involves arranging bricks into rows called

---

BRICKLAYING TECHNIQUES

The basic stretcher bond has been modified to produce stronger walls. The English bond has alternate rows of stretcher bricks (laid with the length parallel to the wall) and header bricks (laid with the short side parallel to the wall). The Flemish bond alternates stretchers and headers in every row.

Stretcher bond

English bond

Flemish bond

courses and sealing them together with mortar to stop rain from getting in. Mortar is a mixture of sand and water with cement, lime, or plaster. Because they are rectangular, bricks can be stacked together in different ways, called bonds.

The simplest way to lay bricks would be to stack them one on top of another, but this would make a very weak wall that would easily collapse. A better method involves laying one row of bricks end to end, then laying the next row on top so each brick partially overlaps the ones underneath. This method is called a stretcher bond. Stronger walls are made by laying some bricks sideways.

Masonry

Craftspeople called masons cut and shape stones before fitting them into place. Basic stone building blocks, known as dimension stones, are generally cut to regular shapes and sizes in quarries to make them easier to work with. Curved, pointed, and other shaped stones may be cut for use on roofs and for decoration.

While bricks can be carefully manufactured so that they are all the same color, stones must be selected from quarried materials so that they are free from marks and other faults. Because suitable stone occurs only in certain places, it usually needs to be transported. Transportation increases the cost of stone, so it is often cheaper and easier to use brick or concrete instead.

Stone is still widely used as a building material, but not always in the form of large blocks. Limestone, for example, is crushed into a powder to make portland cement. This material is used both in masonry work and as a mortar in bricklaying. Artificial stoneware, which may be manufactured from colored concrete, is also widely used for decoration.

CHECK THESE OUT!
✔BUILDING TECHNIQUES
✔CEMENT AND CONCRETE ✔CIVIL
ENGINEERING ✔FOUNDATION

Typical Dutch brick-built city houses. Each region in northern Europe has its own style of domestic brick architecture.

LOOK CLOSER

Cavity wall

Typically, brick buildings are made of not one but two walls, called leaves. These walls are built very close together, with a thin cavity (air gap) between them. The two leaves are held together by wall ties made of metal, usually steel. Older iron wall ties became rusted in around only 20 years. As they rust, ties push the joints apart in the outer leaf of the wall.

The air gap between the leaves helps keep moisture out and acts as a heat insulator, keeping the building cool in summer and warm in winter. Sometimes, the cavity is filled with expanded foam or shredded paper to improve the insulation.

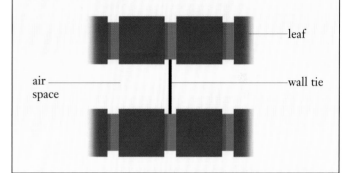

air space — — wall tie
leaf

Bridge

A structure that carries a road, path, or railroad across an obstacle

The Golden Gate bridge in San Francisco.

The earliest bridges were probably trees that had fallen across small rivers. Later, people learned to make their own bridges of wood and stone. Modern bridge builders use wood, steel, and concrete to cross ever wider spaces, creating some of the most graceful of structures.

Bridge basics

A bridge must be able to support comfortably its own weight and the weight of the people or vehicles that cross it. The forces created by these weights will make a weak bridge sag in the middle, and a heavy load crossing it will cause it to collapse. A well-designed bridge transfers these forces safely to the ground through the supports that hold the bridge up.

Bridge builders use a number of methods to make their bridges strong and safe. The simplest is to build one or more supporting pillars, or piers, in the middle of the bridge. Other methods include supporting the bridge on arches and suspending (hanging) it from cables slung between towers at each end.

The type of bridge chosen to cross a gap depends on several factors. The most important of these is the span—the distance that has to be crossed without any support. The height of the bridge is also important if it is to cross a river, road, or railroad. It must be high enough to let boats, vehicles, or trains pass safely underneath. The bridge must also be strong enough to carry the full weight of all the traffic that might use it.

Traditional bridge-building materials such as wood and stone are strong in compression (when pressed together) and tension (when pulled apart). But they are relatively weak when they are bent, and they will snap. This weakness limits the maximum distance that can be bridged by a single wooden or stone beam. A long bridge span made of wood or stone can collapse under its own weight. Bridges made of arches compress each section, instead of bending it. Because of this, it is possible to build relatively wide arches that are made of stone or brick.

During the 18th century, a new range of materials were used in bridge construction. These materials included cast iron, steel, and strong hydraulic (hy-DRAW-lik) cements that harden underwater. Concrete made with these cements provided a new way to set structures in place. Iron, a heavy material, was difficult to support. Steel is an important bridge-building material. It is strong in both compression and tension and is also resistant to bending. Bridges made of concrete reinforced with steel were first built in the 1870s. The first major all-steel bridge

---

HIGHLIGHTS

- ◆ The most common types of bridges are beam bridges and truss bridges.

- ◆ Beam and truss bridges are supported by pillars called piers.

- ◆ Arch bridges are supported by one or more arches.

- ◆ The decks of suspension and cable-stayed bridges hang from thick steel cables.

was the railroad bridge across the Firth of Forth, a river estuary in Scotland. It was completed in 1890. Reinforced concrete and steel are the standard modern materials for bridge building.

Reinforced concrete shrinks as it sets and can continue to do so for up to a year after it is put in place. Concrete arch bridges often have flexible or hinged abutments (structures that hold arches in place). These abutments allow the concrete to change shape slightly as it sets.

Beam bridges

The simplest type of bridge is called a beam bridge. It consists of one or more wooden, stone, or metal beams, supported at each end by piers. The first artificial bridges were almost certainly made of simple wooden planks. In Bronze Age (c. 2000 B.C.E.) Europe, people built raised walkways across swampy ground. These walkways consisted of planks supported by wooden stakes.

Early bridge builders also made beam bridges using stone. They built support piers with piles of stones and laid large stone slabs across them as beams. Some of these ancient bridges, called clapper bridges, can still be found in China, Iraq, and southwestern England. Engineers were still building clapper bridges into the 20th century. These include the Bailey Island Bridge in Casco Bay, Maine, which opened in 1928.

Another type of beam bridge built since ancient times is the pontoon bridge. Instead of having fixed piers, it uses a chain of boats or floating platforms anchored across a river. To cross the Dardanelles Strait from Asia into Europe, the army of the Persian king Xerxes I used a pontoon bridge as early as 486 B.C.E. During World War II (1939–1945), the Soviet armed forces had entire construction divisions dedicated to building pontoon bridges. Most armies still use these structures to cross rivers where there are no bridges or where bridges have been destroyed by enemy action.

A modern beam bridge usually has two or more massive steel girders or concrete beams that are placed side by side across the gaps between the piers. A short bridge needs just two piers, but long bridges may have many more. The steel, concrete, or wooden deck of the bridge sits on top of the girders.

FORCES ACTING ON BRIDGES

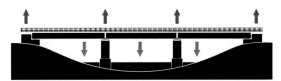

Beam bridge

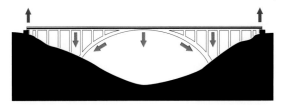

Suspension bridge

Semicircular arch bridge

Segmental arch bridge

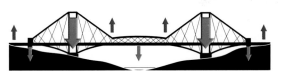

Cantilever bridge

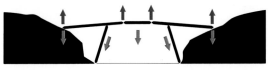

Modern cantilever bridge

The arrows in these diagrams show the forces acting on each type of bridge. Red arrows indicate the powerful downward force of the weight of the bridge. Blue arrows show upward reaction forces countering the weight.

Truss bridges

For extra strength, beam bridges often use structures called trusses instead of simple girders or beams. A truss is a series of interconnected triangles, usually made of steel, that is much more resistant to bending than a solid beam of the same weight. The Italian architect Andrea Palladio (1508–1580) developed the truss bridge around 1570. Using wooden trusses, he built a bridge with 100-foot (30 m) spans across the Cismone River in northern Italy.

Although a truss bridge resists bending movements better than a simple beam bridge, it is more likely to twist in strong crosswinds. To prevent this, the trusses on each side of large bridges are connected together by girders. The girders make the structure much more rigid.

The Pont du Gard, in France, is an arched structure built by the Romans 2,000 years ago. It carries an aqueduct above a road bridge.

A box girder bridge also resists twisting. Instead of solid beams, this type of bridge has hollow rectangular tubes made either of steel or of concrete. These tubes have internal braces to make them stronger. Some highway bridges consist of a single wide rectangular box girder with the road surface laid on top.

Arch bridges

In an arch bridge, the weight of the bridge and the load it carries press against the arch, pushing its bottom ends outward. To prevent this movement, bridge builders dig the bottoms of the arch deep into the ground to hold them safely in place or anchor them in heavy stone, brick, or concrete abutments. The ground, or the weight of the abutments, stops the ends of the arch from moving outward and making the structure collapse. In a long bridge with many arches, the middle arches support each other and the ground or abutments anchor the end arches.

HISTORY

History of bridge construction

c. 3500 B.C.E. The oldest surviving stone clapper bridges are built in Mesopotamia (modern Iraq).

c. 2000 B.C.E. Wooden walkways are constructed across the swampy Somerset Levels, England.

55 B.C.E Romans build a 1,800-foot (550 m) wooden bridge across the Rhine River in Germany.

610 C.E. The An Ji Bridge in Hebei province, China, is the first to use a segmental arch.

1540 The first wooden truss bridge is built across the Cismone River in northern Italy.

1779 English engineer Abraham Darby builds the world's first iron arch bridge, at what is now known as Ironbridge, in central England.

1847 U.S. inventor Squire Whipple designs the first all-iron truss bridge.

1850 The first box girder bridge is built across the Menai Strait in Wales.

1867 The first modern cantilever bridge is built across the Main River at Hassfurt, Germany.

1901 A concrete arch bridge, with hinges to allow for shrinkage, is built over the Inn River in Switzerland.

1977 The New River Gorge bridge, supported on the world's longest steel arch, opens in West Virginia.

1997 The Confederation Bridge, between Prince Edward Island and Canadian mainland, opens.

1998 Japan's Akashi-Kaikyo Bridge, the world's longest suspension bridge, opens.

2000 The 9.5-mile (15 km) Oresund Link, a bridge and tunnel system connecting Denmark to Sweden, opens. It includes the world's longest single bridge carrying both road and railroad traffic.

The Romans built the first arch bridges. They built arches on thick piers so that each arch could stand by itself while neighboring arches were built. This method allowed them to build bridges in stages, moving the supporting scaffolding from one arch to the next as work progressed. The tops of Roman arches were semicircular, so making the arches wider also made them higher. A single semicircular arch covering a large span is very high, so the deck across it slopes steeply up toward the middle. A large number of smaller, lower arches with a flat deck across them avoids this problem. Many arches in a river bridge make it difficult for boats to sail underneath.

The Chinese solved this problem around 610 C.E. by building bridges with segmental arches. The top of a segmental arch is not a complete semicircle, so it is shallower and flatter than the top of a semicircular arch. The first European segmental arch bridge was the Ponte Vecchio in Florence, Italy, built in 1345. The shape of a segmental arch gives a wide span between piers without making the bridge too high. The slopes onto and off a segmental arch bridge are less steep. Because the bridge does not slope steeply, it is far easier for traffic to cross.

Some of the world's most spectacular bridges are huge arches. On some, steel or concrete struts rising up from the arch support a flat bridge running above it. The railroad bridge across the Victoria Falls between Zambia and Zimbabwe, in Africa, is a bridge of this type. On others, steel cables carry a flat, rigid, reinforced deck below the arch. Australia's famous Sydney Harbour bridge was built to this design.

Cantilever bridges

To make a beam bridge, engineers slide or hoist the beams into place on top of the piers. To make an arch bridge, they use scaffolding to support

Disaster on the Tay Bridge

The Tay Bridge disaster of 1879 is a famous example of bridge failure owing to poor design and cost-cutting. The bridge, near Dundee in Scotland, was completed in 1878 and was 2 miles (3.2 km) long—the longest bridge in the world at that time. It had 85 spans, and rose in the middle to 88 feet (27 m) above the Tay River. The central span was 245 feet (74.5 m) long. To save money, the central 13 spans were not properly braced.

On the night of December 28, 1879, a gale-force wind was blowing when a mail train came slowly along the railroad onto the bridge. When it reached the central spans, the weight of the train plus the force of the wind caused a collapse. The train, with a total of 75 passengers and crew, tumbled into the icy waters below. There were no survivors.

the arch during its construction. With a cantilever bridge, they start at the piers and assemble each half of the span piece by piece. Eventually the two halves, called cantilevers, meet to form the complete span. A cantilever is a protruding beam fixed at one end but unsupported at the other. The weight of the securely anchored piers stops the unsupported cantilevers from toppling during construction.

Bridge builders use cantilevers to construct steel truss bridges, concrete beam bridges, and steel or concrete arch bridges. On many cantilever bridges, such as the Quebec Bridge over the St. Lawrence River in Canada, the two cantilevers do not actually meet. Instead, the short gap between them is filled by a length of beam bridge called a suspended span.

Suspension bridges

Instead of sitting on piers, the deck of a suspension bridge hangs from two thick steel cables. The ends of each cable are securely anchored either deep in rock or in massive concrete blocks. The cables pass over two towers, one near each end of the bridge. The bridge deck hangs on smaller cables attached to the

main cables. Long suspension bridges have either stiffened decks or box girder decks so that they do not twist in strong crosswinds. Suspension bridges can span a greater distance than any other type of bridge.

The first large suspension bridges were built at the beginning of the 19th century. They had rigid roadways hung from iron cables or chains and towers made of stone or brick. In the United States, John Roebling (1806–1869) and his son Washington (1837–1926) improved on these designs. In 1889, their most famous bridge, the Brooklyn Bridge, linking Brooklyn with Manhattan, was completed. For this bridge, the Roeblings used steel cables instead of iron.

Steel cables are stronger and last longer than iron ones, and they are used on all modern suspension bridges. Towers are now made of steel and concrete and can carry much more weight than the old stone or brick structures.

The decks of 19th-century suspension bridges often had heavy trusses so that they would be strong enough to carry trains. In the 20th century, automobile traffic became important. Because cars are not heavy, road bridges could be made without trusses and bridge designs became lighter. With lighter decks, suspension bridges could span ever greater distances.

Without stiffening trusses, even a moderate wind could make a bridge sway dangerously. In 1940, a 42-mph (68 km/h) wind blowing across the slim deck of the Tacoma Narrows Bridge, in Washington, made it buck, twist, and then collapse. No more major suspension bridges were built without trusses until the late 1960s, when several bridges with box girder decks were designed.

Cable-stayed bridges

In a cable-stayed bridge, the deck is attached directly to support towers by a number of steel cables. German engineers built the first cable-stayed bridges in the middle of the 20th century. Cable-stayed bridges range in size from small footbridges to very long spans that carry major highways or railroads. Some have cables that spread out at different angles from the tops of the towers. On others, cables run parallel from different heights on the towers. The towers and the decking are made of either steel or concrete, or a combination of the two.

The largest bridge in the United States, and the world's longest cable-stayed bridge, is the Sunshine Skyway Bridge. It has a central cable-stayed structure with shorter spans on each side, each supported by piles. The bridge spans 21,887 feet (6,671 m) over Florida's Tampa Bay.

Movable bridges

Many bridges over rivers can move to allow ships to pass. Some have central sections that rise vertically, pulled by counterweights and electric motors. Drawbridges, such as Tower Bridge in London, England, pivot upward, allowing ships to pass underneath. Swing bridges pivot (turn) horizontally to let ships sail past them.

CHECK THESE OUT!
✔BUILDING TECHNIQUES ✔CEMENT AND CONCRETE
✔CIVIL ENGINEERING ✔ENGINEERING

LOOK CLOSER

Bridging the waves

Some of the longest bridges in the world link islands to the mainland or cross narrow straits of the sea. Two of these remarkable bridges are in Japan. The longest cable suspension bridge in the world is the 6,532-foot (1,991 m) main span of the Akashi-Kaikyo Bridge in Japan. Completed in 1997, this bridge is part of a road and railroad link between Japan's main island, Honshu, and the island of Shikoku. Honshu and Shikoku are also linked by the world's longest double-decker bridge. The Seto-Ohashi Bridge, opened in 1988, is a road and rail bridge, one layer on top of the other. It is 7.6 miles (12.3 km) long, including approaches over land on either side. The longest bridge continuously over sea is the Confederation Bridge, Canada (below). The bridge links Prince Edward Island to the Canadian mainland. It has 44 spans and is 6.8 miles (11 km) long. The waters bridged by its spans freeze each winter, which presented many difficulties for engineers during construction. The Confederation Bridge was designed with several curves rather than being straight. This was to maintain the concentration of drivers using the bridge. The Oresund Bridge, opened in 2000, was built in just seven years. This crossing has two bridges, one of 22 spans and another of 28 spans, and a tunnel. It provides a road and rail link between the cities of Copenhagen in Denmark and Malmö in Sweden.

Building Techniques

Making long-lasting, attractive and useful buildings

This house is being constructed with timber.

Since at least the end of the last ice age (about 10,000 years ago), people have used buildings in which to shelter, live, work, and worship. Over time, different civilizations have developed techniques for making homes and public buildings from a range of different materials.

Working with wood

Wood is widely available and easily worked. It has been a popular building material ever since people developed tools, such as axes and saws, with which to cut and shape it. Wood has been the main building material used by many peoples. For example, most European settlers in 17th-century North America lived in log cabins and timber-framed homes. Elsewhere, wood was used in combination with other materials. In a style of building called half-timbered, a wooden framework of beams was built. The gaps between the beams were filled with bricks and wattle and daub (a mixture of twigs and straw with clay or animal dung).

People have used wood to make many different kinds of dwellings around the world. Enormous timber buildings were constructed in Japan and China 2,000 years ago. The largest surviving examples are the spectacular Buddhist temples in Nara, Japan, which date from the eighth century. The huge, overhanging timber roofs outside these temples are supported by sturdy wooden frameworks inside.

Before iron and steel buildings became popular in the 19th century, builders used wood to make the internal skeletons of many large buildings. This technique is called balloon framing. Today, wood remains a very popular material, and traditional log cabins are built all around the world, from Canada to Switzerland. Some Native Americans make wooden frameworks that are covered by animal

HIGHLIGHTS

◆ Many different materials are used to make buildings, including brick, wood, stone, iron, and concrete.

◆ One of the most widespread modern building materials, concrete, was invented by Roman construction engineers.

◆ Structures such as bridges are carefully designed so they can support more than the maximum weight they might have to carry.

hides to form a tent, or tepee. People living on the steppes of Central Asia build much larger wooden tents called yurts.

Wood is used not just as part of finished buildings, but in two types of temporary structures that are used during the building process. Scaffolding is a type of skeleton that is built outside and around a building to give easy access to the structure and to make construction easier. Although modern scaffolding is usually made from tubular steel, it was once made from poles and planks cut from trees, and this technique is still used in some parts of the world.

Wood is also used in the building technique called formwork. This process uses wooden planks put together to make large molds into which concrete or other building materials are poured and supported while they set.

Building with bricks

Brick is one of the oldest-known building materials and is widely used today. Brick houses were first built 10,000 years ago in southwest Asia. These early bricks were made by pouring a mixture of mud and straw into wooden molds. After drying in the sun, the bricks were stacked and held together with a mud-based mortar (plaster). The houses were topped with a flat roof supported by wooden beams. Bricks were an important part of many Roman buildings, but their use declined following the collapse of the Roman Empire in the 5th century. Brick become popular again in Europe during the 14th century. Today, bricks are widely used across the world, from the flat-roofed mud-brick houses of North Africa and western Asia to the red-brick family homes in the United States and Europe.

HISTORY

Gothic cathedrals

Built in Europe during the Middle Ages, Gothic cathedrals are among the most spectacular stone buildings ever constructed. The architects who designed them wanted to build striking structures that were as tall as possible, but this presented them with many engineering problems. Stone is a heavy material. It was difficult to design buildings with massive walls and roofs that could support their own enormous weight. Architects solved this problem by building arches. Long arches, like tunnels, in the roof are called vaults. Supports that prop the walls were built outside to give extra strength. These massive supports are called flying buttresses.

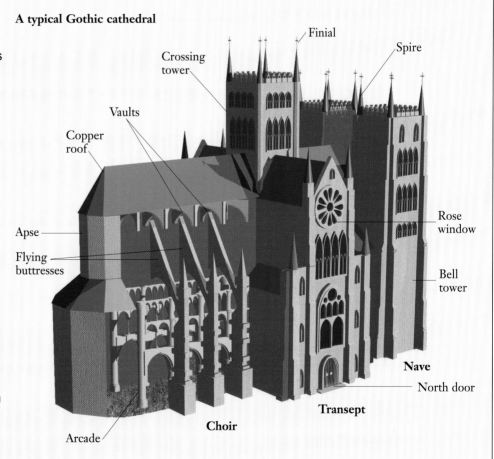

A typical Gothic cathedral

Finial

Spire

Crossing tower

Vaults

Copper roof

Rose window

Apse

Flying buttresses

Bell tower

Nave

North door

Transept

Choir

Arcade

Stone structures

Although stone can be difficult to work and transport, it is one of the easiest building materials to use in places where it occurs naturally. The simplest stone structure is a dry-stone wall. These walls are built from heavy blocks of stone that slot together, piled one on top of another. The weight of the stones holds the wall together without the need for mortar. Early stone houses were built in this way, such as the huts at Skara Brae in Orkney, Scotland, that date from around 2,000 B.C.E. In later buildings, mortar was used to hold the stones together securely and to keep drafts out.

Stone was used to make some of the world's most impressive structures. Around 4,500 years ago, the pyramids of Egypt were built using enormous blocks of limestone, each of which weighed up to 1,100 tons (1,000 metric tons). Greek historian Herodotus (c. 485–425 B.C.E.) suggested that it took at least 100,000 workers 30 years to build the Great Pyramid of Khufu, which stands 481 feet (147 m) tall. This structure was built using only human power. There was no modern construction machinery like cranes or bulldozers to help the pyramid builders.

Stone was used in many other spectacular buildings, notably the great Gothic cathedrals built in Europe during the Middle Ages (between c. 800 and 1500 C.E.). A remarkable surviving example is the huge stone dome built by Italian architect Filippo Brunelleschi (1377–1446) for the Santa Maria del Fiore cathedral in Florence, Italy. This building was completed in 1438. Unlike earlier cathedral domes, Brunelleschi's was designed so that it needed no wooden framework to support it. This technique allowed the dome to be much bigger than earlier works.

Iron and steel

With the 18th-century Industrial Revolution, iron began to be used in place of wood and stone. This strong, durable metal is much easier to use as a building material. Unlike stone and wood, which had to be laboriously cut to shape, iron could be cast into hundreds or thousands of columns or other pieces that were exactly the same size. Iron parts could be produced in steam-powered factories more cheaply than wooden materials. The metal is also much stronger than wood and, while molten, can be worked into arches and other unusual shapes.

Iron became the material of choice for massive constructions during the 19th century. Engineers such as the Englishman Isambard K. Brunel (1806–1859) used cast iron in railroad bridges, stations, and tunnels. One of the most spectacular examples of iron construction was the Crystal Palace, a vast exhibition hall built in London, England, for the Great Exhibition

The Great Mosque of Djenné in Mali is the world's largest mud-brick building.

of 1851. Resembling an enormous greenhouse, this impressive building consisted of thousands of panes of glass mounted on cast-iron columns and arches. It was designed by English architect and gardener Joseph Paxton (1803–1865).

Another cast-iron structure, the Eiffel Tower in Paris, France, was the tallest building in the world on its completion in 1889. This feat of architecture and engineering measured an impressive 984 feet (300 m). French engineer Gustave Eiffel (1832–1923) and his work force managed to assemble the tower in just a few months. The building process was rapid because, like many buildings today, most of the structure was prefabricated (constructed before it was put together) in a factory.

Just as iron largely replaced wood as a structural material in buildings, so iron itself was replaced by steel. Small amounts of carbon and other minerals are added to iron to make steel, which is much stronger. Today, most buildings feature steel in some part of their framework.

Skyscrapers are almost entirely constructed around a basic steel skeleton. Yet this most modern of building techniques dates back to the end of the 19th century, when a pair of Chicago architects, William Holabird (1854–1923) and Martin Roche (1853–1927), constructed the world's first steel-framed building. When the U.S. engineer Elisha Graves Otis (1811–1861) invented a brake that made elevators safe, tall steel-framed buildings became a possibility. This technology led to the shining skyscrapers that now soar above cities around the world.

Concrete and reinforced concrete

Steel may be tough and versatile, but it is not suitable for every type of building. Modern engineering structures, such as bridges and tunnels, are more likely to be made from concrete, a mixture of sand or gravel and cement. Wet and sloppy when first mixed, concrete soon hardens into a tough, long-lasting material. It can be made even stronger if steel bars are placed inside it before it sets. This material is called reinforced concrete. It was used in many major 20th-century building projects, including the Hoover Dam and the TWA Terminal at JFK International Airport in New York.

As well as these engineering marvels, concrete has been used to build homes and offices blocks. Famous architects such as American Frank Lloyd Wright (1867–1959) and Swiss Charles-Edouard Jeanneret (1887–1965; better known as Le Corbusier) used reinforced concrete in many of their most famous buildings. Wright spectacularly demonstrated the strength of reinforced concrete in the headquarters of the S. C. Johnson & Son Corporation in Racine, Wisconsin, which was completed in 1959. Using reinforced concrete, Wright was able to support the building on slender columns only 8 inches (20 cm) wide—roughly a third as wide as the columns in a traditional building.

Concrete may seem like an especially modern material. Yet it was originally used by the Romans, who made it by mixing a type of volcanic ash called pozzolana (pot-zo-LAH-nah) with lime. The material was used in many famous Roman buildings, such as the Colosseum in Rome, the arches and vaults of which are held

Thin reinforced concrete columns support the roof of the Johnson building in Racine, Wisconsin.

together with concrete. The secret of concrete was lost with the fall of the Roman Empire, but the technique was later rediscovered.

The importance of technique

The strength and durability of buildings depend not just on what materials are used but how they are put together. The materials must support loads such as the weight of the roof and the walls. Structures are designed according to the stresses and strains they are likely to be under. Each part of the structure must be strong enough to carry the maximum forces that are likely to be put on it. Thus, a suspension bridge must be able to support not just the weight of the concrete but also the vehicles that drive across it, and it must be stiff enough not to bend too much in the wind. Engineers also allow for extra stress on the structure above the maximum predicted values—this extra margin is called a safety factor.

Through the ages, architects have wrestled with the problem of designing structures that can support a maximum of weight with a minimum of materials. Sometimes, engineers get their figures wrong, and buildings have collapsed as a result. For example, in

Scaffolding is important in the construction of skyscrapers.

LOOK CLOSER

Space frames

In a small building, the outside walls can support the weight of the roof completely. As buildings get larger, inside walls or columns must be added to stop the roof from collapsing. This technique is fine inside a house, where internal walls can be used to separate different rooms from one another. But in factories, sports stadiums, and exhibition halls, internal walls or columns would get in the way.

Modern buildings avoid this problem by using a space frame. Instead of being made of flat concrete or timber, a space-frame roof is made of hundreds of small struts that fit together to make an open pattern of triangles or hexagons. The load of the roof spreads throughout these struts and is safely supported on the walls or columns of the building.

1981 a walkway in a Kansas City hotel collapsed, killing 114 people. Even the strongest building materials will eventually crumble if the structures in which they are used concentrate too much force on their weak points.

Buildings of the future

Buildings have changed dramatically over recent centuries, and they will continue to alter as scientists perfect better materials and engineers dream up new techniques. As people become more aware of the importance of preserving the environment, architects are beginning to design "green" buildings. Some use environmentally friendly materials, such as wood from sustainable forests (plantations where new trees are always grown to replace those that are felled).

Others are shaped to draw fresh air in through the bottom and circulate it throughout the building, saving energy by avoiding the need for air conditioning. Building techniques such as these will continue to be important to ensure that people can live in comfort, safety, and in harmony with the planet.

CHECK THESE OUT!
✔BRICK AND MASONRY ✔BRIDGE ✔CEMENT AND ✔CONCRETE ✔CIVIL ENGINEERING ✔ELEVATOR

Bus

A large motorized vehicle that can carry many passengers

Buses are the most adaptable of all public transportation vehicles. While automobiles can carry only four or five people, buses can carry up to 70. Unlike trains and trams, buses are able to go on any road because they do not have to rely on power lines or rails. Some buses follow scheduled routes in cities or across states. Others are hired for one-time journeys.

Early buses

Today, the school bus is a familiar sight, but buses do not have a long history. Motorized buses began to appear in the United States at the turn of the 20th century. An early example, built by the Mack company in 1904, consisted of a truck chassis (frame and working parts). A freight-carrying truck body was bolted to the chassis during the week, when it served as a truck, and an open-top bus compartment with seats was attached on weekends, when the vehicle carried passengers. The first actual bus chassis was made in California in 1921. Five years later, a U.S. company built the first bus that enclosed the passenger-carrying section and the engine within a single frame.

Modern buses

Modern buses are quieter and more comfortable. Some of the most sophisticated buses are used on transcontinental routes. With air conditioning, video players, and rest rooms, they offer levels of comfort similar to those found on airplanes. Typically streamlined and made from light materials, these transcontinental buses can travel faster than ordinary buses.

Some buses are designed to cater to disabled or elderly people. "Kneeling buses" have suspension systems that can be lowered automatically at the curb so that passengers do not have to climb steps. They also have room for wheelchairs and baby strollers.

Modern buses are also more environmentally friendly than buses of the past. In some buses, the engine's power is transmitted to the wheels indirectly. A diesel or gasoline engine drives a generator that, in turn, supplies power to an electric motor that drives the wheels. On city streets, just electric power is used.

Buses of tomorrow

Tomorrow's advanced buses may be like the Environmental Concept Bus (ECB) developed by Swedish manufacturer Volvo in 1995. With a battery-powered engine for stop-start driving in the city and a gas engine for motoring quickly through the suburbs, the ECB saves a great deal of energy and produces little pollution. **The ECB's roof-mounted headlights are also** radically different from conventional vehicle lighting. Using ultraviolet light, these headlights seem invisible to people but they show the road markings, pedestrians, and animals more clearly than normal lights.

Greater use of buses, as part of planned transportation systems for cities, could be an important way to reduce gridlock (traffic congestion). In many cities, buses drive in lanes that only they are allowed to use, sometimes guided between low concrete barriers.

CHECK THESE OUT!
✔ELECTRIC ROAD VEHICLE ✔POLLUTION
✔ROADS ✔STEAM ENGINE

Greyhound buses serve more than 2,600 U.S. and Canadian destinations.

Cable, Electrical

Conductors that carry electricity

Electrical cables deliver electric power from its source to the machines, lights, and other equipment that use it. In the home, the cables that connect the lights and power outlets each have two or three separate wires inside. These wires are called conductors because they conduct (carry) the electric current.

Covers for cables

Domestic wiring cables usually have copper wire conductors, but some have aluminum conductors. Each conductor has plastic covering as insulation (material that does not conduct electricity). The insulation prevents the flow of electrical current between the conductors, a condition called a short circuit. A short circuit can trip (operate) automatic switches called circuit breakers, which protect an electric circuit from overload.

Distribution cables

Cables that bring electricity to houses have much bigger conductors because they carry a lot more power. In city centers, these distribution cables are underground. In less populated areas, they are carried above the ground on wooden poles.

Inside an underground distribution cable, each copper or aluminum conductor has an insulating covering. Some cables have plastic insulation around conductors and layers of plastic and steel wire armor to protect the conductors from damage. A plastic outer layer keeps moisture from seeping in. In the most widely used types of underground cables, the conductors are insulated by layers of tough paper tape soaked in oil. Tape also wraps the conductors together, and they are

HIGHLIGHTS

◆ The wires inside cables are called conductors.

◆ Underground cables and cables in buildings have insulated conductors.

◆ Overhead power lines usually have bare conductors but are covered with plastic near trees.

enclosed inside a flexible sheath of lead, aluminum, or bronze. A protective outer layer of plastic covers the sheath, and the cables may also be armored with steel wire or steel tape.

Overhead distribution cables carried on poles are usually bare copper or aluminum conductors. Glass or porcelain insulators support each conductor. Insulators prevent electricity from passing through the pole to the ground and hold the conductors apart to stop them from short circuiting. Some cables have a plastic covering to stop them from touching tree branches.

Transmission cables

Electricity travels from power plants to distribution systems through transmission cables. Transmission cables in cities are normally buried underground, but outside cities they are carried on tall steel towers, or pylons.

CHECK THESE OUT!
✔ELECTRICITY ✔ELECTRICITY TRANSMISSION
✔ELECTRONICS ✔FIBER OPTICS

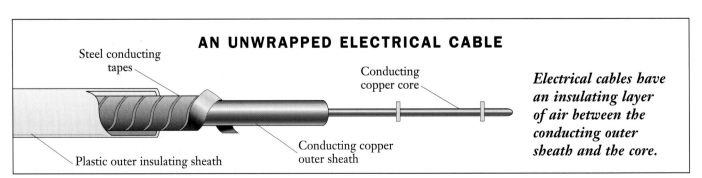

AN UNWRAPPED ELECTRICAL CABLE

Steel conducting tapes

Conducting copper core

Plastic outer insulating sheath

Conducting copper outer sheath

Electrical cables have an insulating layer of air between the conducting outer sheath and the core.

Canal

An artificial channel for carrying goods and passengers by water

Before the invention of railroads and motor vehicles, boats on canals and rivers often provided the easiest way to transport heavy freight. As well as carrying boats, canals can simply move water from place to place to fill reservoirs, drain swampy land, or to irrigate (water) farmland. Some canals, such as the Panama Canal in Central America and the Suez Canal in Egypt, are large enough for ocean-going ships to navigate.

Some natural waterways (rivers and lakes) are deepened, widened, or straightened to make it easier for boats to use them. Others are extended by digging canals to link rivers, lakes, and the ocean. The first canal builders dug channels through low-lying ground to link rivers

HIGHLIGHTS

♦ A canal is an artificial water-filled channel.

♦ Most canals are built for boats to sail on, but some move water from place to place to fill reservoirs, to drain swamps, or to water farmland.

♦ Canals can cross hills and valleys using locks, tunnels, and aqueducts.

♦ Some canal systems use inclined planes or elevators as alternatives to locks.

Up to eighty ships, such as this aircraft carrier, pass through the Suez Canal, Egypt, each day. But some bulk carriers and supertankers are too large for passage.

or other natural stretches of water. They did this to create new transportation routes. Because the water supports the weight of a boat and its load, canal boats could be pulled by horses or teams of workers walking along the bank.

Ancient Egyptian canals date from as far back as 2000 B.C.E., and the Romans built extensive canal systems in Italy, France, the Netherlands, and England. In Europe, canal construction ended with the fall of the Roman Empire in the 5th century, but it revived in the 12th century. By the 18th century, Europe had an extensive network of canals. In the United States, there were more than 4,000 miles (6,400 km) of canals in use by the end of the 19th century.

Building canals

Most canals were built long before the invention of modern earth-moving equipment such as bulldozers and diggers. To cut a canal trench, hundreds of people dug by hand for months or even years. Before explosives were available, they often had to cut through solid rock. Today, canal projects need fewer workers because they use modern construction equipment and explosives.

Canals must be lined to stop the water from leaking into the ground. Early canal builders used clay mixed with water to make a waterproof putty called puddle. They plastered puddle onto the bottom and sides of the canal trench to make a lining up to 3 feet (1 m) thick. To protect the lining from the impact of boats, they covered the canal sides with wooden beams or brick walls. Modern builders line canals with concrete because it is both waterproof and strong.

The completed channel is filled with water by diverting nearby rivers. Unlike a river, a canal has no natural source of water, so it must always have a good supply, such as a river or reservoir, to keep it topped up.

Rises and descents

The designers of a canal try to keep its route on level ground. Sometimes this is impossible, so canal builders have developed several ways of

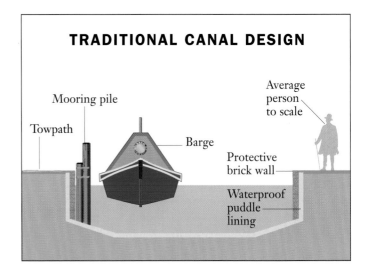

TRADITIONAL CANAL DESIGN

Mooring pile

Towpath

Barge

Average person to scale

Protective brick wall

Waterproof puddle lining

dealing with slopes and hills. When there is a slight rise in the ground, they cut the trench deeper to keep the canal bed horizontal (flat). Where the surrounding land slopes away, they build raised embankments on either side of the channel to keep the water in. They often build these embankments with dirt and rocks dug up elsewhere along the route of the canal.

Hills and valleys are more difficult to deal with. When a hill has steep slopes, it is often easier to bore a tunnel than to dig a deeper trench. Tunneling is also needed if the canal has to pass through built-up areas. For example, Regent's Canal in London, England, runs through a long tunnel beneath houses that were built before the canal was dug.

To carry canals across steep valleys, canal builders often use an aqueduct (AK-wuh-dukt), which is a bridge that carries water in a watertight trough. Old aqueducts were built with stone or iron, but modern ones are made from steel or concrete. Aqueducts also take canals across roads, railroads, and rivers.

Locks

A canal cannot go down a long, gradual incline (slope) without the water running out at the lower end. Canals descend slopes in a series of separate flat stages, like the steps of a staircase. The steps, short lengths of canal, are usually formed by a flight (series) of locks—structures that allow boats to pass through in either direction. The most common type of lock, a gate lock, consists of a chamber with a set of movable gates at each end. These gates prevent water from flowing from the upper stages of the lock into the lower ones.

When a boat moves from an upper stage into a lower one, water from the upper stage flows into the chamber through doors in the lock gates or through large pipes that are built into the sides of the canal. When the water level in the lock chamber is the same as the water level in the upper stage, the gates between the chamber and the upper stage open. The boat then moves into the lock chamber, and the gates close behind it.

Next, another set of sluices opens to allow water to flow out of the lock chamber into the lower stage of the canal. The water level in the chamber drops down again. When it reaches the same level as the water in the lower stage, the gates between the chamber and lower stage open. The boat moves out of the chamber and into the lower stage. When a boat wants to move from the lower of the two stages to the upper one, the

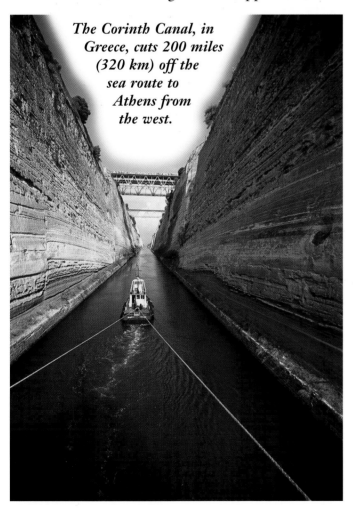

The Corinth Canal, in Greece, cuts 200 miles (320 km) off the sea route to Athens from the west.

HOW A LOCK WORKS

Upper gate

When a boat needs to move downstream, the upper gates are opened to admit it to the lock. The lower gates remain closed.

Lower gate

Once the boat is inside the lock, the upper gates are closed. The sluices in the lower gates are opened to release water from the lock and lower the boat.

When the water inside the lock has reached the lower level, the lower gates are opened, and the boat slowly moves out of the lock.

Sluices

The lower gates are then closed, and the sluices in the upper gate return the lock to its original state.

whole process is reversed. Most locks have a pair of gates at each end. The combined width of a pair of gates is about 10 percent greater than the width of the lock, so that when they close they form a V. Each gate forms an angle of about 60 degrees to the lock wall. The pressure of water on the V helps hold the gates closed. On smaller canals, the lock gates are opened and closed by hand, but the big, heavy gates on large canals need hydraulic or electrical power to move them.

Alternatives to locks

A boat is sometimes moved from one stage of a canal to another on a slope called an inclined plane. The boat is hauled out of the water and is

HISTORY

The history of canal construction

c. 2000 B.C.E. Egyptian pharaoh Sosostris orders the building of a canal connecting the Nile River and the Red Sea. It falls into disrepair but is restored by the Persian king Darius I around 500 B.C.E.

c. 215 B.C.E. The Chinese emperor Qinshihuang orders the construction of the Ling Chhu, or Magic Canal, the first canal to be built through land of varying height.

c. 600 C.E. Work begins on the 1,110-mile (1,770 km) Grand Canal linking the Chinese cities of Tianjin and Hangzhou.

1642 The first European transportation canal with gate locks is completed. It runs between the Loire and Seine Rivers in France.

1681 The 150-mile (240 km) Canal du Midi in southern France connects the Mediterranean Sea to the Garonne River, allowing barges an easy route from the Mediterranean to the Atlantic coast.

1761 The Bridgewater Canal opens in England. It carries coal from mines into the city of Manchester. The canal incorporates 46 miles (74 km) of underground tunnels, which allow barges to go straight to the coal face.

1824 Completion of the 363-mile (580 km) Erie Canal linking the Great Lakes with New York City.

1834 The Philadelphia-Pittsburgh Canal is completed. A huge set of inclined planes carry it over the 2,334-foot (711 m) Allegheny Mountains.

1869 French civil engineer Ferdinand de Lesseps completes the Suez Canal, in Egypt, linking the Mediterranean and Red Seas.

1887–1895 Building of the Kiel Canal, in Germany, which connects the North Sea to the Baltic.

1893 In Greece, the Corinth Canal links the Aegean and Ionian Seas. Restarted in 1882, the project was first attempted by Roman emperor Nero in 67 C.E.

1914 The Panama Canal, designed by U.S. engineer John F. Stevens, is completed. The canal links the Atlantic and Pacific Oceans.

1959 The U.S.- and Canadian-funded St. Lawrence Seaway opens, improving the connection between the Great Lakes and the Atlantic Ocean.

1992 The Europa Canal in Germany is completed. It links the Main and Rhine rivers to the Danube, and creates a 2,200-mile (3,500 km) waterway stretching from the North Sea to the Black Sea.

placed on sets of wheels that run on rails. Electric- or diesel-powered winches pull the boat up, or lower it down, the slope. Alternatively, the boat may be floated into a large, water-filled tank called a caisson (KAY-suhn), which is hauled up and down the slope as required.

To save power, some inclined planes are wide enough to take two boats moving in opposite directions on separate tracks. A system of chains and pulleys links the two so that the weight of the boat moving down the slope helps raise the one coming up. If there is only one boat, an empty caisson is filled with water to balance it. The Morris Canal, built in the 19th century

to carry coal from the Delaware River to New York City, had 23 inclined planes with locks between them. The highest part of the canal was 990 feet (300 m) above the lowest part. On the Philadelphia-Pittsburgh Canal, a bigger series of inclined planes were constructed to carry boats over the 2,334-foot (711 m) Allegheny Mountains. This canal was completed in 1834.

In 1968, a large inclined plane was built on the renovated Charleroi-Brussels Canal in Belgium. It is nearly 1 mile (1.6 km) long and rises 220 feet (67 m). There are two caissons, each 300 feet (90 m) long. These caissons can raise or lower a 1,490-ton (1,325 metric ton)

Europa barge, the standard European barge, in around only 20 minutes.

The steepest inclines

Where there is a very steep rise between two levels, some canal systems have elevators to lift caissons. These elevators generally have two caissons, so that the caisson going down helps raise the one going up.

The biggest modern canal elevators are in Germany. The largest is on the Elbe Lateral Canal, at Scharnebeck. Completed in 1976, it carries Europa barges in tanks weighing up to 6,300 tons (5,700 metric tons) through a height of 126 feet (38 m). The elevator's tanks are counterbalanced by 224 concrete disks.

Canal boats

Canal boats have to be narrow because they have to fit through canals. So, to carry a lot of cargo, canal boats are also very long. Because canals are not very deep, a canal boat has a shallow draft, meaning its bottom is not far below the water surface. Some traditional canal boats, called narrow boats, are around 7 feet (2.1 m) wide. Other modern-day canal boats,

Lock gates allow some water to pass through to prevent pressure building up.

called barges, are larger, measuring at least 14 feet (4.2 m) across.

In the early days of canal transport, most canal boats were horse-powered. One of the barge crew led a horse along a path at the side of the canal, called the towpath. The horse pulled the boat along with a line attached to its harness. When traveling through a tunnel, where there was often no room for a towpath, the horse was untied and led overland. The rest of the crew lay on their backs on top of the barge. Then they drove the barge through the tunnel by pushing their feet against the walls and roof of the canal tunnel.

By the beginning of the 20th century, horsepower was replaced on most canals by small steam, diesel, or electric locomotives. These locomotives ran along railtracks beside the towpath. On other canals, the boats were powered by onboard engines. Almost all modern-day canal boats are powered by these engines, which usually run on diesel.

CHECK THESE OUT!
✔CIVIL ENGINEERING ✔DREDGING
✔PORT ✔SHIP AND BOAT

LOOK CLOSER

The St. Lawrence Seaway

The St. Lawrence Seaway was built jointly by the United States and Canada to connect the Great Lakes to the Atlantic Ocean. It is a good example of a modern waterway that is based on a modified river. The St. Lawrence River was dredged to a depth of 27 feet (8 m), and deep-water channels were dredged through all of the Great Lakes. Work on the seaway began in 1954, and it opened in 1959.

Because today's ships are larger, and because the seaway is closed every winter by ice, the number of ships using it is falling slowly. The construction of the canal was disastrous for the Great Lakes' environment. Many nonnative species invaded the lakes through the seaway. Zebra mussels began to outcompete native shellfish, and lampreys also arrived—they feed by ripping holes in the bodies of other fish and drinking the blood.

Cancer Treatments

Techniques used by doctors to tackle cancer

Cancer is a serious illness that affects more than one million people in the United States every year. It is caused when part of a person's body starts to grow very quickly, often forming a lump called a tumor. If tumors are allowed to keep growing, they can begin to damage healthy parts of the body. Tiny sections of the tumor may break off and spread to other parts of the body via the blood, causing new tumors to grow elsewhere. The tumors stop the body from working properly and make the cancer sufferer very ill, and sometimes they cause death.

The uncontrolled growth of cancerous tumors can be triggered by agents called carcinogens (KAR-sin-uh-juhnz). Many of these agents are chemicals. Some occur in cigarette smoke, others in environmental pollution. Radiation, such as X rays and ultraviolet light, and viruses (tiny disease-causing agents) can also cause cancer.

Help at hand

Doctors use several treatments to stop tumors from causing damage to the body. About a half of the people who are discovered to have cancer in the United States receive treatment that either cures them completely or helps them live for many years more. Each type of cancer causes a distinct series of health problems, and doctors use a different pattern of treatments to control them. If the tumor is small or is discovered early, treatment aims to eliminate the cancer before it causes damage or spreads elsewhere. If the cancer has already spread or has caused extensive damage, treatment focuses on tackling the suffering but does not try to remove the cancer.

Surgery

Most cancer sufferers are treated using surgery at some point during their illness. A surgeon operates by slicing carefully into a patient and cutting away the tumor. The patient is given drugs that make them sleep during the surgery. The surgeon uses a very sharp knife, called a scalpel, to make precise cuts. However, if the tumor is on or near the surface of the body, the surgeon may freeze it first with liquid nitrogen. Tumors that are in the rectum and colon (the end of the digestive system) are usually burned away using lasers, and some cancers are cut away using hot electric wires. Surgery is an effective

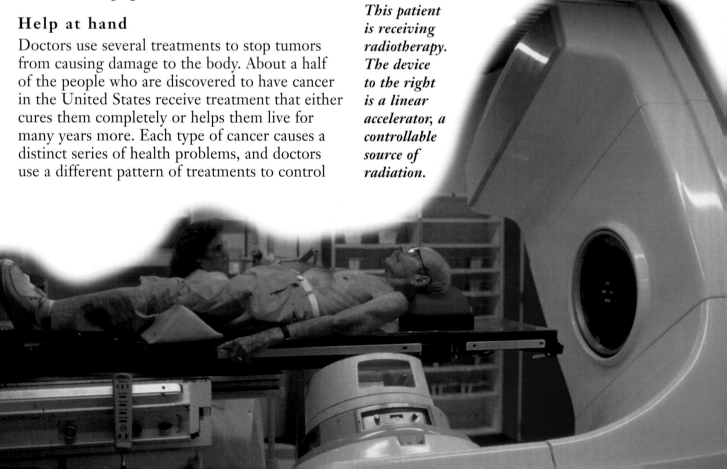

This patient is receiving radiotherapy. The device to the right is a linear accelerator, a controllable source of radiation.

cancer treatment. Nevertheless, other treatments are used before and after surgery to ensure the cancer sufferer has the best chance of recovery.

Hot rods and rays

Tumors inside the body can sometimes be treated by firing beams of radiation into them. This treatment is called radiotherapy. It is often used after surgery to destroy parts of the tumor that the surgeon missed, or in place of surgery on tumors that cannot be reached easily.

Radiotherapists (people who treat cancers with radiation) aim thin beams of radiation at the tumor from different angles. The beams cross each other inside the tumor, killing the cancerous cells. The single beams that travel into and out of the body are so weak on their own they do not cause damage to the healthy parts of the patient's body.

Sometimes, rods of radioactive metal are placed near the tumor. These rods release radiation, which kills all the surrounding tissue, including the tumor. Radiotherapy can cause people to lose their hair and feel tired and sick. Radiotherapy is given in small doses over several weeks to minimize these side effects.

INTO THE FUTURE

Confusing cancer cells

In 2001, scientists made a major breakthrough in cancer treatment. Using a technique called gene therapy, the scientists fooled cancer cells into activating genes—packages of inherited information that determine how a cell develops—that allow the cells to be destroyed. Most cancer cells switch on a gene called telemerase, which allows them to keep dividing indefinitely. The scientists took the trigger for the telemerase gene and attached it to a second gene, called nitroreductase.

The cells were tricked into activating this second gene, which is an effective cancer treatment. It works by changing a harmless drug into a cancer-cell killer. Normal cells are unable to switch on either gene, and so they are unharmed by the treatment. Gene therapies like this one promise to save many lives from cancer in the future.

HIGHLIGHTS

◆ Cancer treatments attempt to remove dangerous growths called tumors.

◆ Surgeons cut out the tumors using a scalpel or may burn them with lasers.

◆ Beams of radiation are aimed at tumors to reduce them in size.

◆ Chemotherapists use a cocktail, or mixture, of medicines to fight cancer.

Cancer medicines

Using medicines to treat cancer is called chemotherapy (KEE-moh-ther-uh-pee). There are many medicines that destroy cancers, and they are also used to stop tumors from spreading. Tumors that spread are called malignant, while those that grow in one place are called benign. Chemotherapists use a cocktail of medicines to destroy as much of the cancer as possible.

Some cancer medicines are designed to attack cancer cells that are dividing and multiplying. These medicines also attack healthy cells that are dividing, such as bone marrow cells and cells in the roots of hairs. As a result, chemotherapy produces side effects, such as hair loss and blood diseases. Doctors may add medicines that reduce these side effects to the chemotherapy cocktail.

Biological therapies

A patient's immune system can also be used to fight cancers. Interferons (in-TUHR-fir-ahnz) are chemicals made by the body that make white blood cells destroy cancer cells. Interferons have been injected into cancer patients. Sometimes, the interferons are successful, but the side effects are often severe. Scientists are also working with antibodies to fight cancer. Antibodies are chemicals that stick to certain cells. Antibodies could be used to deliver medicines directly to cancer cells, leaving healthy tissue alone.

CHECK THESE OUT!
✔MEDICAL IMAGING ✔PHARMACOLOGY ✔SURGERY

Casting

The process of casting is like making ice cubes—a liquid is poured into a mold. In the case of ice cubes, water is poured into cavities in a plastic tray. When the water freezes, it becomes a solid object that is the same shape as the cavity. In casting, the liquid used is molten metal, molten glass, concrete, or plastic resin (REZ-un; a natural or artificial liquid). The mold cavity is the same shape as the object to be made, such as a car engine block or a plastic toy.

Many industries use casting to create a wide range of objects, from the individual teeth of a zipper to steel girders for construction sites or the huge propellers of ocean liners. They make these objects by pouring molten material into heat-proof molds. When the material cools and hardens to become solid, it takes on the shape of the cavities in the molds.

Metal casting

Factories that make metal castings are called foundries. They use molds shaped so that molten metal can fill every part of them and then be removed easily when it has become solid. Most large metal castings are made by pouring molten metal into a mold of fine sand, in a process called sand casting. To make a mold, foundry workers

Molten metal pours into a row of identical molds. Large numbers of castings are made in reusable molds in industries such as the automobile industry.

HIGHLIGHTS

◆ In sand casting, molten metal is poured into molds made of sand.

◆ In die casting, molten metal is injected into steel molds and cooled quickly.

◆ Investment casting uses wax patterns that are melted away by the liquid metal.

pack fine, damp sand around a full-size wooden or metal model of the casting, called a pattern. Then they remove the pattern, and the imprint it leaves behind in the sand forms the cavity of the mold. Sometimes the sand is mixed with clay to help it keep its shape. When the mold is ready, the workers pour in molten metal, taking care that it flows into all parts of the cavity.

When the new casting has cooled, the workers remove it from the mold and clean it. Sometimes the surface is machined to make it smoother. The surface of the casting is rough because of the roughness of the inside of the sand mold. Mixing the sand of the mold with a resin instead of clay makes its inside surface much smoother. Using resin is more expensive, but it produces smoother castings that need less machining. Also, sand-resin molds can be used several times before they need to be refashioned—molds of sand or sand-clay can only be used once.

Molds made of metal are more expensive to make but are cheaper to use since they can be used over and over again. These molds are usually made of steel. They are coated in resin to keep the molten metal from sticking to them.

Die casting

Instead of simply pouring molten metal into a mold, die casting involves its injection under pressure into metal molds called dies. Once injected, the molten metal solidifies quickly in the die, which is often cooled by water. Then

LOOK CLOSER

Metal Casting in the United States

The first foundry in what is now the United States was the Saugus Iron Works, near Lynn, Massachusetts. It began operation in 1642. Other colonies along the eastern seaboard soon had foundries of their own. Foundries were important in the early development of American industry, and many foundry workers played key roles in the American War of Independence (1775–1783). Patriot Paul Revere operated a foundry, and seven other foundry operators signed the Declaration of Independence on July 4, 1776.

Today, foundries supply components to every major manufacturing industry in the United States, including energy, transportation, agriculture, aerospace, and national defense. There are around 3,000 U.S. foundries. They employ nearly 200,000 people and make roughly 14 million tons (12.7 million metric tons) of castings each year. The metal casting industry is the largest recycler in the United States. Around 20 million tons (18 million metric tons) of scrap metal and more than 100 million tons (91 million metric tons) of sand are recycled every year.

Some of the largest castings made are the propellers of supertankers.

the die is opened and the casting is ejected from the cavity. Die casting is a high-speed process, because injecting the metal takes much less time than pouring it. It also produces high-quality castings that normally do not need further machining. Automobile manufacturers use die casting to make components such as engine blocks, valve covers, and the casings for alternators and steering columns.

Investment casting

In investment casting, the pattern that creates the mold cavity is made of wax. Foundry workers cover the pattern with layers of a liquid ceramic or plaster mixture that hardens when it dries. This process creates a hard shell around the pattern. Molten metal poured into the shell melts the wax, which runs out though a hole in the bottom of the mold. The metal flows into the shaped cavity left behind by the melted wax.

Investment casting, also called the lost-wax process, is an ancient casting method. Both the Greeks and the Romans used it to create magnificent bronze sculptures. Although it has such a long history, investment casting was not widely used in industry until World War II (1939–1945). Investment casting also uses materials such as plastics and even frozen mercury, as well as wax, to produce objects ranging from the heads of golf clubs to medical equipment, and from weapons to jewelry.

Other types of casting

Centrifugal casting creates hollow shapes such as pipes by pouring molten metal into a rotating mold. The rotation of the mold forces the metal outward against the wall of the mold cavity, where it hardens. Objects made of glass, plastic, and concrete can also be cast. Plastic objects are made by pouring plastic resin into aluminum molds. This technique, called liquid-resin casting, is used to produce toys, medical equipment, and plastic components for electronic equipment.

CHECK THESE OUT!
✔IRON AND STEEL ✔METALS ✔PLASTICS

Catalyst

Reactions occur when certain chemicals, or reactants, are combined. Catalysts are substances that speed up these reactions but remain unchanged by them. Although some catalysts do react during the process, they always re-form and can be used in further reactions.

Groups of catalyst

Industrial scientists divide catalysts into two main groups, the heterogenous (het-uh-rah-JEE-nyus) catalysts and the homogenous (hoh-muh-JEE-nyus) catalysts. Heterogenous catalysts are of a different physical state from the chemicals in a reaction. For example, if the chemicals involved in the reaction are liquids, a heterogenous catalyst may be a solid or a gas. By contrast, homogenous catalysts are in the same state as the chemicals in a reaction. If the chemicals are liquids, a homogenous catalyst is also a liquid.

How heterogenous catalysts work

Most heterogenous catalysts are transition metals, a large group of elements that includes common metals such as iron, nickel, and copper. Some of the most important heterogenous catalysts are rare, expensive transition metals, such as platinum, gold, and palladium. Most substances consist of different elements bonded together (linked) in a compound. For example,

table salt is formed through bonding between sodium and chlorine. Molecules are the smallest naturally occuring particles of a substance. Heterogenous catalysts attract molecules of the reactants to their surfaces. The catalyst weakens the bonds of the reactants and brings the molecules together so new bonds form.

Homogenous catalysts

Homogenous catalysts work in a different way. They form temporary compounds with the reactants, which then break down into the end products. The catalyst, though, returns to its original form once the reaction is complete. All sorts of organisms rely on homogenous catalysts to help speed up processes such as digestion, heat production, and even light production. Biologists call these natural catalysts enzymes (EN-zims).

Catalysts in industry

Most industrial processes depend on catalysts. Heterogenous catalysts are widely used to make bulk chemicals. These chemicals are important because they are the starting materials for many other products, such as fertilizers and detergents. Homogenous catalysts are involved in reactions to make smaller amounts of high-value products, such as electrical parts, perfumes, and medicines. Some enzymes are used in the production of foodstuffs.

Solid catalysts, such as transition metals, form weak bonds with the reactants, holding them close to their surfaces. They work best when they have a large surface area, because more of the reactants can come into contact with the catalyst to react. Catalysts are often riddled with tiny holes, called pores. These pores are introduced by chemists to increase the surface area.

HIGHLIGHTS

- ◆ Catalysts are substances that speed up chemical reactions without being chemically altered.

- ◆ Homogenous catalysts are in the same physical state as the chemicals in a reaction.

- ◆ Heterogenous catalysts are in a different physical state from the chemicals in a reaction.

- ◆ Catalyst performance can be improved by increasing the surface area.

catalysts. Hydrogen atoms are added to carbon-containing molecules with the help of metal catalysts, such as nickel. Hydrogenation is an essential part of margarine manufacture, turning vegetable oils into solid fats.

Petroleum, oil, and catalysts

Minerals called zeolites (ZEE-oh-LYTS) are important catalysts in the petroleum industry. Zeolites contain elements such as silicon, aluminum, and oxygen. These elements are joined in a honeycomb structure, giving the zeolite a large surface area. A process called cracking uses powdered zeolites as a catalyst.

Cracking involves breaking up the long chains of hydrocarbons (molecules containing carbon and hydrogen) that make up crude oil into smaller, lighter molecules. The lighter molecules are easier to burn and are used as fuel in automobiles and airplanes.

CHECK THESE OUT!
✔BIOTECHNOLOGY ✔OIL REFINING ✔ POLLUTION

Chemical plants use heterogenous catalysts in the bulk manufacture of their industrial products.

Powdered catalysts spread over supporting materials greatly increase the surface area. Many catalysts are rare and valuable, so it is often important to make a little catalyst go a long way.

Catalysts at work

German chemist Fritz Haber (1868–1934) was one of the first scientists to use catalysts in industry. In 1909, Haber developed a method to produce ammonia gas from nitrogen and hydrogen using an iron oxide catalyst. Called the Haber process, this was an efficient way to make large quantities of ammonia, an important component of fertilizers and explosives.

Catalysts also help industrial chemists make polymers (PAH-luh-muhrz), a group of materials that includes plastics. By using catalysts, chains of ethylene (eth-uh-LEEN) molecules join together at lower temperatures than would otherwise be possible. The resulting polymer, polyethylene, is used to make a wide range of plastic products.

Hydrogenation (hi-drah-juh-NA-shuhn) is another important industrial process that uses

---

LOOK CLOSER

Catalysts and the environment

Catalysts are important for conserving natural resources and protecting the environment against pollution. Since catalysts reduce the heat and pressure needed to make reactions work, their use can lead to huge energy savings. They can also reduce the amounts of by-products produced by chemical reactions.

Today, most new automobiles, buses, and trucks are fitted with catalytic converters. As the engines of these vehicles process fuel, they release exhaust fumes, gases that contain polluting gases including hydrocarbons and carbon monoxide. Catalytic converters break down these waste products into less harmful gases, such as water vapor and carbon dioxide. Inside a catalytic converter, exhaust gases pass through filters coated with catalysts. These filters are made of the metals platinum and rhodium. These metals speed up the chemical reactions between the pollutants, breaking them down and allowing new compounds to form.

Cement and Concrete

Strong, tough, low-cost materials used in construction worldwide

Around 2000 B.C.E., Egyptian and Babylonian builders began to use a material resembling cement to hold their temples and other great public buildings together. Cement is a mixture of lime, a naturally occurring chemical, with materials that contain the minerals silica and alumina. Lime becomes a powerful adhesive (sticking substance) when mixed with water.

Around 100 B.C.E., Roman inventors produced a cement that sets underwater, by mixing lime with volcanic ash and water. When the Roman Empire collapsed in the 5th century C.E., the secret of making cement was lost with them. English engineer John Smeaton (1724–1792)

HIGHLIGHTS

◆ Cement and concrete are materials commonly used in the construction industry.

◆ Cement is a mixture of lime with materials rich in silica and alumina, such as clay or ash.

◆ Concrete is a mixture of cement, water, and aggregates such as sand or crushed rocks that increase its volume.

◆ Most modern cement is called portland cement, after its similarity to a type of limestone found in Portland, southern England.

MAKING PORTLAND CEMENT

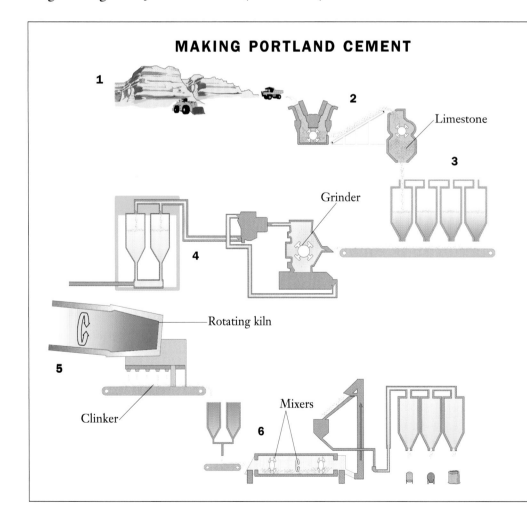

1. *Limestone is quarried (dug).*
2. *Quarried limestone is crushed in a two-stage process.*
3. *Limestone is mixed with crushed shale (rock made of fine particles), sand, and iron ore (rock that contains iron).*
4. *The powder is ground and blended.*
5. *The mixture is loaded into a rotary kiln. When it is heated, it partly melts to form clinker.*
6. *Clinker is mixed with gypsum before being ground to form cement. The cement is stored, bagged, and shipped.*

LOOK CLOSER

Reinforced and prestressed concrete

Concrete's strength under tension can be reinforced by pouring it around metal bars, rods, or steel mesh. Concrete binds around the metal and then expands and contracts at the same rate as the metal as the temperature rises or falls. Reinforced concrete can withstand forces caused by vibrations and bending. It is used in bridges, skyscrapers, and other large structures. Prestressed concrete is a reinforced concrete that can withstand great tension but is relatively lightweight. Prestressed concrete is placed under permanent compression using steel wires once it has set. It can be made in two ways. In pretensioning, steel wires are laid in an empty mold, stretched, and then secured firmly before the concrete is poured in. In post-tensioning, concrete is poured with channels running through it. Steel wires are then run through the channels.

rediscovered the process in 1759 while he was developing materials to build the Eddystone Lighthouse in the English Channel.

The most widely used modern cement was developed in 1824 by English bricklayer Joseph Aspdin (1799–1855). The cement looked like limestone quarried (dug) at Portland in southern England, so it was named portland cement.

How portland cement is made

The main ingredients of portland cement are limestone or chalk, which contains lime, and a material rich in silica and alumina, such as clay or ash. The finished cement also contains a mineral called gypsum (JIP-suhm), as well as iron oxides. The materials are crushed and ground into powder and then blended together.

The mixture is then heated to high temperatures in a rotary (rotating) kiln to form a dense, hard material called clinker. When the clinker is cool, it is ground into a fine powder and mixed with gypsum before being sealed in airtight bags. The addition of gypsum is important, since it releases water while the cement sets, keeping it fluid longer.

Making concrete

Concrete is formed when cement and water are mixed with another material, such as sand, to increase their volume. Owing to its strength and toughness, concrete is among the world's most widespread building materials. Concrete also has the advantage of being relatively cheap. Today, concrete is used to construct a wide variety of structures, including walls, floors, beams, pipes, tanks, roads, bridges, and dams.

Preparing concrete involves three steps: mixing, laying, and then hardening under controlled conditions. Cement is mixed (by hand, in a portable mixer, or in a truck with a rotating drum) with materials such as sand or rock, and water is added. The less water used, the stronger the concrete. Once the water is added, concrete is poured into molds called forms. To prevent it from cracking or shrinking, the concrete is left to set in controlled conditions. Concrete has great strength under compression, when squeezed or pressed down. Yet it is quite weak under tension (when it is stretched) and also when twisted or bent. Some specialized concretes, including precast, reinforced, and prestressed concrete, are used to minimize these weaknesses.

CHECK THESE OUT!
✔ BRICK AND MASONRY
✔ BUILDING TECHNIQUES
✔ CONSTRUCTION SITE

The Romans used cement to build the gladiators' amphitheater, the Colosseum, in Rome.

Centrifuge

A rotating machine that separates different ingredients in a mixture

A centrifuge (SEN-truh-fyooj) is a device that spins objects or materials at very high speeds to separate heavy substances from lighter ones. Swedish engineer Carl de Laval (1845–1913) developed the first centrifuge in 1878. His machine was designed to separate cream from milk. Centrifuges soon found their way into laboratories and factories. By around 1920, researchers were using them to separate blood cells from plasma, the liquid part of blood. Today, researchers and industrial chemists use centrifuges to remove impurities from substances. Scientists also use them to separate different substances in mixtures for analysis.

How a centrifuge works

The most familiar centrifuge is the domestic spin dryer. It has a metal drum perforated with small holes. The drum spins around at high speed. The spinning flings the clothes outward and presses them against the wall of the drum. The water in the wet clothes is squeezed out through the holes. The clothes are flung by a force called centrifugal (SEN-truh-fyoog-uhl) force.

Industrial and laboratory centrifuges use centrifugal force to separate mixtures. The mixture might be one of large particles mixed up with finer powder, or of particles mixed into

HIGHLIGHTS

◆ The first centrifuge was a cream separator that was constructed in 1878.

◆ Large centrifuges help prepare astronauts for the g-forces they encounter during rocket launch.

◆ The fastest centrifuges can create forces millions of time stronger than the force of gravity.

a liquid. It could also be a mixture of two or more different liquids or gases. In a typical laboratory centrifuge, a cross-shaped rotor spins at high speed within a stationary casing. The casing prevents people from touching the rotor and catches anything that might accidentally fly off from the rotor. Small bottles called test tubes contain the mixture to be separated. The tubes sit in holes at the ends of the rotor arms.

When the rotor spins, the tubes tilt horizontally with their bottoms pointing outward. The centrifugal force has a stronger effect on the heavier parts of the mixture than on the lighter ones. It pushes the heavier parts outward, forcing them to the bottoms of the tubes. When the centrifuge stops, and the test tubes tilt upright again, the heavier substances settle at the bottoms of the test tubes with the lighter ones above. Laboratory technicians can then carefully draw off each separate layer.

Centrifuges in industry

Centrifuges that use test tubes process material in small batches. Industry often needs continuous processing, and to do this a tubular centrifuge is used. This machine is a tall tubelike vessel that rotates at high speed like a vertical roller. Liquids pumped into the top of the tube pass down through it. They separate rapidly in the spinning tube and are removed continuously by pumps. Some industrial centrifuges use perforated drums similar to domestic spin dryers to filter solids

PEOPLE

Theodor Svedberg

Swedish chemist Theodor Svedberg (1884–1971) developed the first ultracentrifuge in 1924. To eliminate friction (a rubbing force) between the rotor and the surrounding air, which limits the speed of the rotor, he pumped all the air out of the centrifuge casing. He also built the casing of transparent material so that he could watch the substances in the tubes gradually separate. Svedberg won the Nobel Prize for chemistry in 1926. And to further honor his work, the rate of separation of large molecules is now measured in svedberg units.

from liquids. The solids stick to the inside of the drum, and the liquids are forced through the holes. The mining and food processing industries often use this type of centrifuge.

Space agencies such as NASA use a type of centrifuge to train astronauts. This device has a chamber mounted at the end of a horizontal arm. Trainee astronauts strap themselves into the chamber, and the arm begins to rotate, whirling the chamber around in circles. The centrifugal force acting on the astronauts is similar to the apparent force of gravity (or g-force) endured by astronauts when a spacecraft is launched.

Ultracentrifuges

In some laboratory centrifuges, test tubes sit at a fixed angle in the rotor. The centrifugal force pushes the heavier parts of the mixture against the sides of the tubes as well as toward the bottom. Very high speed centrifuges, called ultracentrifuges, often use this arrangement and spin at more than 20,000 revolutions per minute.

In 1937, scientists used an ultracentrifuge to separate chlorine gas into its isotopes (EYE-suh-TOHPZ). Isotopes are forms of an element that are chemically the same but have a slightly different mass (amount of matter). The separation of these chlorine isotopes was an important early use of centrifuges. Modern-day laboratory scientists use both ultracentrifuges and the slightly slower high-speed centrifuges to separate out different gas isotopes.

Nuclear scientists use ultracentrifuges to produce weapons-grade uranium to make nuclear warheads. They convert uranium into a gas and then separate out the isotopes they need.

U.S. scientist Jesse Beams (1898–1977) invented a magnetic suspension system for the rotor of ultracentrifuges. This invention reduced the influence of friction on the centrifuge even more, allowing the rotor to spin much more quickly. Today, high-performance centrifuges can be less than 0.4 inch (10 mm) across and can rotate at up to a million revolutions per minute. This speed creates a centrifugal force five million times greater than the force of gravity.

Biological cells contain a number of different subunits called organelles. These organelles include the nucleus, which contains genetic (inherited) information, and the mitochondria, which produce energy. Biologists often need to separate out these organelles for analysis. The best way to do this is with an ultracentrifuge.

CHECK THESE OUT!
✔CHEMICAL INDUSTRY ✔FOOD TECHNOLOGY
✔WASHING MACHINE AND DISHWASHER

This centrifuge is used by NASA to test the influence of gravity on biological samples.

Ceramics

Hard materials formed by fusing powders at high temperatures

Most people think of ceramics as the dishes and bowls used in homes for cooking or serving food. Pottery and bricks are two kinds of ceramics that have been used by people for thousands of years. In modern times, many types of ceramics are made and put to a wide range of uses. Modern ceramics include the spark plugs in a car engine, the materials used by dentists to repair teeth, parts of computers, and even the thermal tiles that protect the space shuttle.

Three main groups of materials are used in engineering. These groups are metals, polymers (PAH-luh-muhrz; compounds such as plastics), and ceramics. Ceramics are the best materials to use when an object needs to be both strong and able to withstand very high temperatures, or when it needs to provide electrical insulation.

Ceramics are easily molded and can be finished using a process that is known as glazing. Glazing gives the ceramic product a smooth surface that is easily cleaned. For these reasons, and because they can withstand heat, ceramic products such as bowls and plates are widely used to cook and serve both food and hot drinks.

How are ceramics made?

The word *ceramic* comes from the Greek word *keramikos*, which means "potter's clay." Like clay, ceramic materials must be baked to make them tough and strong. Ceramics are rigid and lightweight. Although they may contain metallic substances, ceramics are not classed as metals. Unlike metals, they do not conduct electricity. Unlike soft polymers and plastics, ceramics are hard, but they are also more brittle. Modern ceramics are made using both mixing and baking processes. They contain a wide range of materials that help determine how they are used.

The first step in ceramics manufacture is to make a powder from one or more compounds. The elements in the compounds may be metallic, such as aluminum, silicon, and zinc, or nonmetallic, such as oxygen, carbon, and nitrogen. Most ceramics include some of each.

The ceramic tiles that cover the nose of the space shuttle are made from a very light material called foam glass. This material is manufactured from pure silica and liquid chemicals that are microwaved until they are hard.

A liquid, called a binder solution, is then added to the powder to produce a mixture called a slurry. Slurry contains fine, insoluble (nondissolving) particles in water. The mixture is soft and can be poured into molds that are formed to give the required shape.

Next, the firing process gives the material permanent shape and makes it strong and rigid. Firing usually takes place in a kiln (oven), where temperatures can reach thousands of degrees. Inside the hot kiln, the powder grains fuse together to form strong chemical bonds (links).

Changes in firing times and temperatures and the presence or absence of pressure during the firing can produce ceramics with varying numbers of tiny holes called pores. Ceramics that contain many large pores are bigger in volume, but are also weaker, than ceramics that have fewer or smaller pores. Porous ceramics (ceramics that fluids can soak through) are widely used in the chemical industry.

Modern ceramics

Ceramics are now found in some surprising places. They are used in many high-technology industries, for example, as chip carriers inside computers and other electronic equipment. These carriers hold the computer chips and their electrical connections. Ceramics are used for this purpose because they are very good insulators (they do not conduct electricity).

The thermal tiles that protect the hull of the space shuttle are made of ceramic material. They are designed to withstand the enormous

---

INTO THE FUTURE

Ceramic engines

In the past, metal parts in automobile and truck engines corroded, melted, or wore out quite quickly. These problems have been partly overcome by coating moving parts, such as piston rings and bearings, with ceramic material. In the future, it is possible that whole parts in engines, not just coatings, will be made of ceramics, particularly if ones can be developed that are less brittle.

Metal parts in engines must be lubricated (made slippery) with oil to prevent them from seizing up because of the heat produced by friction (rubbing). The metal parts must also be cooled using water and radiators, or they will melt with use. Replacing metal parts such as rotors, rings, and pistons with ceramic materials means that engines will last longer. Ceramics are lighter than metals, so they will also help cut down on weight and thus save energy.

---

temperatures generated when the vehicle reenters Earth's atmosphere. These ceramic tiles are also strong enough to survive the stresses of the shuttle's takeoff and landing. The tiles are fixed to the underside, nose, and along the leading edges of the shuttle's wings.

Limitations of ceramics

Although they are very useful and have a very wide range of applications in science, in industry, and in the home, ceramics do have some drawbacks. Their main limitation is brittleness, which causes them to shatter when subjected to a force. Metals and polymers absorb stress by warping or bending. Ceramics cannot do this. They stay rigid until they break. Designers and engineers must consider this drawback whenever a design involves a load being placed on a ceramic material, such as in a building or bridge, for example. Another limitation is that ceramics are often porous, which gives them a rough surface that may need to be smoothed off.

CHECK THESE OUT!
✔BRICK AND MASONRY ✔CEMENT AND CONCRETE
✔METALS ✔SPACE FLIGHT

HIGHLIGHTS

◆ Ceramics are one of the three main groups of materials used in engineering. The other two groups are metals and polymers.

◆ Unlike metals, ceramics do not conduct electricity, and, unlike polymers, they are hard.

◆ The main drawback of ceramics is that they are brittle. This property has restricted their use in the manufacturing and construction industries.

Chaos Theory

The idea that some systems are unstable and can change in unexpected ways

Many apparently simple systems behave unpredictably, or chaotically (ka-AHT-ik-lee), over long time periods. Study of this unpredictability in the mid-20th century led to the development of chaos (KA-ahs) theory, which was originally used to describe the unpredictability of weather systems. Chaos theory today is applied to many other systems, in biology, medicine, and economics.

Understanding chaos theory

Systems such as the weather are chaotic. They are sensitive to minute changes. A tiny difference in the original conditions of a chaotic system dramatically alters its development. Change may be small at first, but it becomes increasingly disruptive, eventually causing chaos.

A famous example of chaos theory in action is called the "butterfly effect." Chaos theory suggests that a tiny initial disturbance, such as the fluttering of a butterfly's wings, can alter the future of a large-scale weather system. The tiny air current produced by the butterfly could eventually determine whether a raging hurricane will form thousands of miles away several months later.

According to chaos theory, the fluttering of the wings of a small butterfly could, in time, lead to a powerful hurricane thousands of miles away.

Chaos theory was partly discovered by U.S. weather expert Edward Lorenz (1917–). In 1961, Lorenz learned how sensitive weather was to tiny changes when he ran a weather prediction computer program. Running the complex program many times, Lorenz tried to save time by trimming the figures he fed in by two decimal places. He thought that such tiny changes would not affect the end results greatly. To his surprise, Lorenz found that the new results varied wildly from previous predictions: altering the starting conditions had drastic long-term effects.

HIGHLIGHTS

◆ Chaos theory explains why many different systems behave unpredictably.

◆ Chaotic systems are sensitive to initial conditions. A tiny change in the original state of the system may have a "knock-on" effect that results in chaos.

◆ Chaos theory was first applied to weather systems. This theory is now important in many other fields, such as economics and medicine.

Chaos in other fields

Scientists have discovered that heart attacks may be governed by chaos theory. A tiny change in the regularity of the heartbeat can have a catastrophic long-term effect, resulting in a heart attack. In economics, chaos theory explains how tiny variations in stock exchanges and currency (money) markets may have a "knock-on" effect and eventually cause whole systems to crash.

While chaos theory highlights the difficulty of long-term prediction, it can be useful to planners in identifying areas in which unexpected large variations are likely to occur. This can allow safeguards to be designed.

CHECK THESE OUT!
✔MEASUREMENT ✔METEOROLOGICAL INSTRUMENTS

Chemical and Germ Warfare

Weapons that attack the workings of the human body

Chemical and biological weapons attack the body and prevent it from functioning properly. Chemical weapons are nonliving substances that poison the body. Biological weapons are living organisms, such as bacteria, used in germ warfare to cause diseases.

Sting in the air

Chemical weapons were first used in Europe, during World War I (1914–1918). The most infamous chemical weapon was mustard gas. Soldiers exposed to mustard gas choked to death if they could not protect themselves by wearing gas masks and protective clothing.

Biological weapons were also used during World War I, when the microorganisms that cause glanders, a horse disease, were released by both sides to reduce the number of horses available for enemy cavalry and transportation.

Modern weapons

Chemical and biological weapons were not used in World War II (1939–1945), but governments continue to develop ever deadlier types. For example, sarin, a colorless and odorless gas, is lethal to people in minute amounts.

During the Gulf War (1991), allied soldiers wore protective suits against chemical or biological attack.

Most chemical weapons are nerve gases. These gases disrupt the way signals from and to the brain are sent through the body. Some nerve gases can be absorbed through the skin and so cannot be stopped by gas masks alone. Iraq fired nerve gas against Iranian forces in the 1980s, and members of a Japanese religious cult released sarin gas in the Tokyo subway in 1995.

Spreading diseases

Several countries have stores of infectious bacteria and viruses that can be spread on the wind to cause diseases. Although a gas mask can protect people from biological weapons, they are harder to detect than chemical weaponry. The bacteria that cause the disease anthrax have been tested by scientists from several nations. In the form of a white dust, anthrax has been used to attack people. In 2001, envelopes containing anthrax were sent through the U.S. Postal Service. Although officially eradicated by 1980, cultures of the smallpox virus are believed to be maintained by several countries.

HIGHLIGHTS

◆ One of the earliest chemical weapons was mustard gas.

◆ Most chemical weapons are nerve gases.

◆ Organisms that may be used in germ warfare include the smallpox virus and anthrax bacteria.

CHECK THESE OUT!
✔BOMB AND SHELL ✔CHEMICAL INDUSTRY
✔NUCLEAR WEAPONS

Chemical Engineering

Design and construction of large chemical plants

Chemical engineers design, build, operate, and maintain industrial plants that produce chemicals. These plants include oil refineries, petrochemical plants that make chemicals from oil, and plants for making drugs and medicines. Most chemical engineers construct new plants or keep existing plants running smoothly.

Designing a chemical plant

There are three main stages in chemical production. The first involves preparing raw materials for processing. This might involve grinding and dissolving solid materials, or vaporizing (turning to gas) liquids. The second step is the processing itself, which takes place in equipment called reactors. Inside the reactors, catalysts (substances that speed up chemical reactions) are often used to make the chemicals quickly. The third stage involves the separation of these chemicals from the mixture in the reactors and then purifying them.

The components inside a chemical plant include reactor vessels, distillation columns, heat exchangers, and pipes, plus control equipment such as valves, pumps, and sensing equipment. Sensing equipment detects and monitors temperatures and pressures and the amount of material flowing through the system.

The importance of size

Sometimes, engineers have to design a chemical plant for a process that already works well in other plants. Their main task is to decide the size of the equipment. The starting point is the amount of product the plant will make in a given time. The engineers must calculate how much material will have to flow into and through the system. They must also figure out how much heat energy will be absorbed or released at different stages of the process. These calculations are known as mass and energy balances. These basic data describe what happens in the plant.

From the mass balance, engineers calculate how much material will pass through each piece of equipment, which determines how big the equipment needs to be. From the energy balance, the engineers locate places in the system where material needs to be heated or cooled. This information tells them how much heat and power the system will need. Armed with all this data, the engineers can figure out what sizes of pipework and pumps they need to carry the materials through the system.

Designing a new process

To design a plant to make a completely new product, or to use a new process to make a familiar one, is more complicated. This work begins in a research laboratory, where industrial chemists discover new products and the reactions that produce them. The lab process, however, makes only a few ounces or grams of the product at a time. Industrial plants must make hundreds or thousands of tons each year. Chemical engineers have to scale up the lab process into a full-size plant. They also have to change the system from making a single batch at a time to producing a continuous flow of the product.

Scaling up for industry

Scaling up the process can bring unexpected problems. For instance, a reaction may produce little heat in the lab but a dangerous amount in a full-size plant. This heat might be enough to vaporize the materials, raise the pressure, and cause an explosion. Alternatively, the process might not work at all when scaled up. Chemical engineers scale up the lab process in several stages, gradually increasing the amounts of

Many large modern chemical plants are on the coast because imported oil is the principal raw material.

raw materials in the chemical reactors. The information gained in these stages helps engineers decide how to remove the finished product from the reactors and purify it and what types of equipment they will need to use.

When this stage of the research is complete, engineers use the data to design and build a pilot plant. This machinery is a reduced-scale chemical plant that uses smaller versions of the equipment that the final plant will have. It allows the engineers to try out the process and ensure that it works properly. These trials also produce samples of the product for testing. For example, the pharmaceutical industry uses pilot plants to make samples of new drugs. The samples are tested to make sure they are safe to use.

The full-scale process can differ from the lab process in many ways apart from size and continuous production. These differences affect the final design of the chemical plant. For instance, lab processes normally use pure raw materials. The purity of the materials simplifies the chemical reactions so that researchers can study them more easily. Industrial plants are designed to use materials with more impurities because they are cheaper.

Heat and pressure problems

Another difference is that most laboratory reactors work at atmospheric pressure, but industrial plants often use pressurized reactors. In the laboratory, a gas burner provides the heat, but in industry the heat often comes from coils of tubing filled with hot water, oil, or steam.

Catalysts in lab reactions are often dissolved within the raw materials. Industrial plants prefer solid catalysts because they are easier to remove from the finished products.

Engineers rarely have to design new reactor vessels. They can usually use customized (made-to-measure) versions of standard reactors. These reactors include continuously stirred tanks for reactions with liquids and vessels for reacting gases together.

Another type of reactor, called a fermenter, handles biochemical reactions. Biochemistry is the branch of science that deals with the chemistry of living organisms. Biochemical reactions involve tiny living organisms such as

In June 1974, a huge explosion destroyed the chemical plant at Flixborough in eastern England. The disaster had far-reaching effects on chemical engineering practices in the United States, Europe, and elsewhere. The Flixborough plant made caprolactam, one of the main ingredients of a type of nylon. In March 1974, engineers shut the plant down for routine maintenance. The engineers took one of the reactors out of service and bypassed it with a length of pipe and flexible rubber tubing. The pipe and tubing connected the reactors on either side of the one that was out of service. Then, the engineers started up the plant again and pressurized and heated the working reactors.

On the afternoon of June 1, a freak pressure wave blasted through the bypass system and destroyed it. More than 50 tons (45 metric tons) of hot cyclohexane (SY-khlo-HEK-san), a chemical as flammable as gasoline, escaped from the reactor system and instantly vaporized. A cloud of cyclohexane vapor rose into the air. Less than a minute later, the cloud reached the flare units at the top of the plant and exploded with devastating force. Fire raged across the site for 25 minutes, with flames reaching more than 300 feet (90 m) into the sky. The flames created a windstorm as the air rushed in. The blast flattened 90 percent of the buildings on the site, injured more than 400 people, and killed 28. The cause of the pressure wave that triggered the disaster is still unknown.

After the disaster, countries around the world brought in strict new safety rules for chemical plants. These rules covered the design and operation of chemical plants handling dangerous substances and those using pressurized equipment.

Devastation at Flixborough caused by the explosion of a cloud of flammable cyclohexane gas.

bacteria and yeast. Fermenters contain a mixture of raw materials and the organisms that create the biochemical reactions, plus the products.

Choosing the right materials

When the engineers have designed the chemical plant, they have to choose materials to make the equipment. These materials must be able to cope with high temperatures and pressures. They also have to resist corrosion (being worn away) by the chemicals used in the process. Laboratory reactions use glassware, as it is resistant to corrosion by all but the most powerful acids, but glass is not strong enough to use in industrial plants. Instead, engineers use steel vessels, pipes, and valves. These are lined where necessary with corrosion-resistant materials. Food and drug plants use equipment lined with hygienic, nontoxic (nonpoisonous) materials such as glass or stainless steel.

CHECK THESE OUT!
✔CHEMICAL INDUSTRY ✔FOOD TECHNOLOGY
✔OIL REFINING ✔PHARMACOLOGY ✔VALVE

Chemical Industry

The production of chemicals for use in industry and in the home

There are two main types of chemicals: organic and inorganic. Organic chemicals are based on carbon. They are used to produce a vast range of products, from dyes and glues to plastics and explosives. Most inorganic chemicals are not based on carbon. They include the acids and salts that are essential raw materials for many industries and the fertilizers used in agriculture.

History of organic chemicals

Early uses of organic chemicals in industry, such as using animal fats to make soap, date back to ancient times. The modern organic chemical

U.S. chemical plants, such as this one, contribute 10 percent of the nation's exports.

HIGHLIGHTS

◆ Organic chemicals are compounds of carbon. Scientists now know at least 14 million organic compounds.

◆ The organic chemical industry uses a few simple building-block chemicals to make thousands of different products.

◆ Polymers are made from around one half of all the organic chemicals produced.

◆ Most inorganic chemicals are not based on carbon.

◆ Sulfuric acid, an inorganic chemical, is the leading product of the whole chemical industry.

industry began in the 19th century. Before then, many scientists thought that chemicals from organic beings (from animals and plants, and their remains) could not be made artificially.

In the 19th century, chemists discovered that organic chemicals could be manufactured. At first, their main raw material was coal tar, a complex mixture of substances created as a by-product when coal is heated.

English chemist William Perkin (1838–1907) was working with coal tar when he accidentally discovered the first synthetic dye in 1856. The discovery of this dye, called mauveine, was a landmark in the development of the organic chemical industry. Throughout the industrialized world, chemists began to experiment with coal tar, searching for dyes and other useful chemicals. Coal tar remained the chief source of raw materials for organic chemicals until around 1950. Today, more than 90 percent of organic chemicals are produced using oil or natural gas, though much of the rest comes from coal tar.

Organic compounds

The raw materials obtained from oil and natural gas are simple organic compounds. A compound is a combination of two or more basic chemical substances, or elements. For instance, water is a compound made of the elements oxygen and hydrogen. Organic compounds are made of carbon combined with other chemical elements, such as hydrogen. Compounds made of carbon and hydrogen are called hydrocarbons. The hydrocarbons are an important group of chemicals that includes most of those made from coal tar, oil, and natural gas.

Producing organic chemicals

The organic chemical industry takes simple compounds made from oil and natural gas and builds them up into more complex compounds. In this way, thousands of different types of substances can be produced.

The process begins in an oil refinery. Crude oil is converted into gasoline, diesel oil, and lubricating oil. Some oil is converted into simple building-block chemicals such as ethylene (eth-uh-LEEN), propylene (PRO-puh-LEEN), xylene (ZI-LEEN), and toluene (tuhl-ya-WEEN). These are the raw materials of the organic chemical industry. Another important building block, methane, comes from natural gas. Together, these compounds are usually called heavy organic chemicals because millions of tons are produced each year. Making chemicals from the basic building blocks may take one reaction, or several reactions may be required. To make styrene (sti-REEN), the starting material for polystyrene plastic, one reaction converts benzene into ethylbenzene (eth-uhl-BEN-zeen) and a second converts that into styrene. Making drugs and dyes is complicated and may involve processes of several steps.

LOOK CLOSER

Polymers

The large group of chemicals known as polymers (PAH-luh-muhrz) are among the most important products of the organic chemical industry. Like all materials, they are made up of billions of atoms. An atom is the smallest possible amount of a pure chemical element. Atoms of an element join together to form molecules (MAH-lik-KYOOLZ) of that element. They also join up with the atoms of other elements to form molecules of chemical compounds.

Polymers are very large molecules, much larger than the molecules of most other substances. They consist of hundreds or thousands of smaller molecules, called monomers (MAHN-nuh-muhrz), linked together in long chains. The monomers may all be the same kind of molecule or they may be of two or more different kinds.

Some polymers, such as starch, are natural. Others, such as nylon, polyethylene, and other plastics, are synthetic (artificial). Plastics are very useful materials because their long polymer chains make them strong and flexible. As well as using polymers to make plastics, the organic chemical industry uses them to make a wide range of synthetic fibers, synthetic rubber and elastic, and surface coatings and glues. Other specialized types of polymers include thickeners used in processed foods and the superabsorbent materials in disposable diapers. Around one half of all organic chemicals produced end up in synthetic polymers.

Organic compounds that are difficult to make are obtained either from plants or by the action of single-celled microorganisms such as bacteria and yeast. These compounds include starch (an important foodstuff also used as glue), cellulose (a substance that strengthens the walls of plant cells), proteins (the building blocks of cells and organisms), and antibiotics, which kill bacteria. Today, scientists know more than 14 million organic compounds.

Inorganic chemicals

Most chemicals not based on carbon are called inorganic. The exceptions are a few simple carbon compounds, such as carbon dioxide, which are classed as inorganic, although they do contain carbon. Many inorganic chemicals are compounds of metals, but pure metal production is not part of the inorganic chemical industry.

Although the use of inorganic chemicals dates back thousands of years, there was no real understanding of them until the Industrial Revolution in the 18th century. Early pioneers included Antoine Lavoisier (1743–1794) from France and John Dalton (1766–1844) from England. Lavoisier made the first proper list of chemical elements. He also discovered that when substances burn, they combine chemically with oxygen in the air. Dalton revived an ancient Greek theory that all matter is made of tiny particles called atoms. He also discovered that chemical elements form compounds when their atoms combine with those of other elements.

Methods for analyzing chemicals became more accurate during the 19th century. The introduction of electrolysis (ih-lek-TRAH-luh-suhs; breaking down substances using electricity) was a major breakthrough. Using electrolysis,

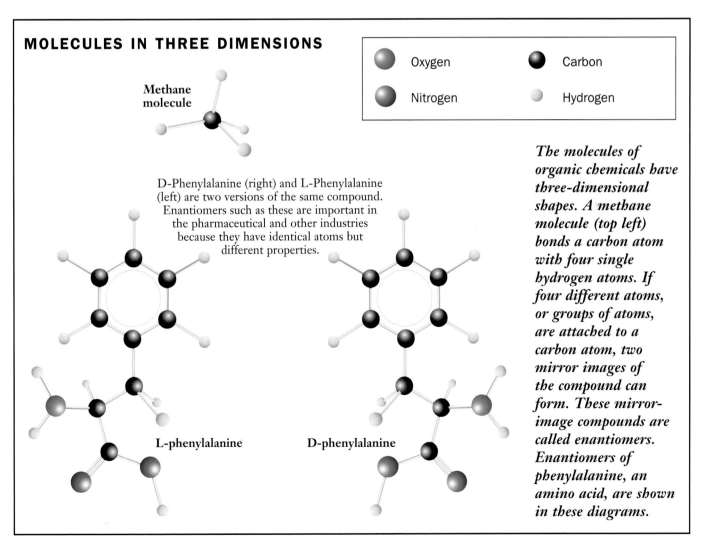

MOLECULES IN THREE DIMENSIONS

Oxygen
Carbon
Nitrogen
Hydrogen

Methane molecule

D-Phenylalanine (right) and L-Phenylalanine (left) are two versions of the same compound. Enantiomers such as these are important in the pharmaceutical and other industries because they have identical atoms but different properties.

L-phenylalanine

D-phenylalanine

The molecules of organic chemicals have three-dimensional shapes. A methane molecule (top left) bonds a carbon atom with four single hydrogen atoms. If four different atoms, or groups of atoms, are attached to a carbon atom, two mirror images of the compound can form. These mirror-image compounds are called enantiomers. Enantiomers of phenylalanine, an amino acid, are shown in these diagrams.

scientists could isolate and study many more substances than before. At the same time, there was a rapid growth of new industrial processes. This led to increased demand for the chemicals these processes required.

Today, the organic chemical industry is one of the inorganic industry's best customers. For example, most of the chlorine (KLOR-EEN) from the inorganic industry goes to make the organic plastic PVC (polyvinyl chloride; PAH-LEE-vi-nuhl-KLO-RYD).

Producing inorganic chemicals

The value of the inorganic chemical industry is more than $18 billion in the United States and $90 billion worldwide. Much of this value comes from inorganic chemicals that are produced in bulk, such as acids, alkalis (AL-kuh-lys; compounds that react with an acid to form a salt), ammonia (a gas that is a compound of nitrogen and hydrogen), and chlorine. With millions of tons produced each year, these are called heavy inorganic chemicals.

Acids

Inorganic acids are known as mineral acids. Sulfuric, nitric, and hydrochloric (hy-dro-KLOR-ik) acids are the most important industrial mineral acids. They all react strongly with other substances and have many different uses in the chemical industry.

In terms of tonnage produced, sulfuric acid is the leading product of the entire inorganic chemical industry. This acid became important

HISTORY

Early Advances in the Chemical Industry

1648 German physician Johann Glauber discovers hydrochloric acid.

1746 English inventor John Roebuck devises the lead chamber process for producing sulfuric acid.

1772 Swedish chemist Karl Scheele discovers oxygen. English chemist Joseph Priestley, who is usually credited as the discoverer, identified this gas two years later.

1789 French chemist Antoine Lavoisier publishes his *Elementary Treatise on Chemistry*.

1789 In France, Count Claude Louis de Berthollet discovers that chlorine can be used as a bleach.

1791 French chemist Nicolas Leblanc patents a method of making soda (sodium carbonate) from salt and sulfuric acid.

1804 English chemist John Dalton publishes his atomic theory.

c. 1810 The rapid growth in the use of coal gas for lighting leads to the production of large amounts of coal tar.

1834 Friedlieb Runge in Germany and Michael Faraday in England independently produce hydrocarbons from coal tar.

1856 English chemist William Perkin discovers the first synthetic dye. Named mauveine, it was manufactured from coal tar.

1865 Belgians Ernest and Alfred Solvay invent an improved way of making soda.

1865 German chemist August Kekulé von Stradonitz discovers the atomic structure of the hydrocarbon benzene.

1909 Belgian-born U.S. chemist Leo Baekeland produces Bakelite, the first plastic.

1913 The world's first ammonia plant opens in Oppau, Germany. It produces ammonia by the Haber-Bosch process, devised by German scientists Fritz Haber and Karl Bosch.

Buckminsterfullerene

In 1985, a molecule shaped like a soccer ball and made up of 60 carbon atoms was created. The newly discovered molecule was called buckminsterfullerene (BUHK-MIHN-stuhr-FOO-luh-REEN) because its structure looks like one of the domed roofs designed by U.S. architect Richard Buckminster Fuller (1895–1983). Buckminsterfullerene is one of a group of carbon compounds called fullerenes. These compounds created great excitement because they act as superconductors. Superconductors are almost perfect conductors of electricity since they offer no resistance at normal temperatures.

during the 18th century for converting salt (sodium chloride) into soda (sodium carbonate) for soap making. Today, the single biggest use of sulfuric acid is in making phosphate- and nitrogen-based fertilizers. It is also used in car batteries, the manufacture of paper, synthetic rubber, plastics, and paints, and pickling (cleaning) steel to remove rust.

Nitric acid is mainly used to make ammonium nitrate fertilizer, by reacting the acid with ammonia. Nitric acid is also used to make dyes, plastics, explosives, and many other products. In industry, hydrochloric acid began as an unwanted and dangerous by-product of making soda from salt. Today, this acid's major uses include pickling steel and producing gelatin (a gel-like substance derived from animal tissues), soy sauce, and high-fructose syrup (a sweetener made from glucose).

Alkalis

Alkalis are chemical opposites of acids. When an alkali mixes with an acid, they neutralize each other and form a chemical salt plus water. Most industrial alkalis are compounds that contain sodium and potassium. Sodium hydroxide (caustic soda) has many industrial uses, including making paper, soap, and detergents. Sodium carbonate (soda or washing soda) is a chief raw material for making glass and is useful as a cleanser, a disinfectant, and a water softener. The most important potassium compound is potassium hydroxide (caustic potash), used to make an ingredient of liquid detergents. Ammonia, a compound of nitrogen and hydrogen, is an important alkali used in the fertilizer and explosives industries.

CHECK THESE OUT!
✔CHEMICAL ENGINEERING ✔FUELS AND PROPELLANTS ✔OIL REFINING ✔PHARMACOLOGY ✔PLASTICS ✔RUBBER

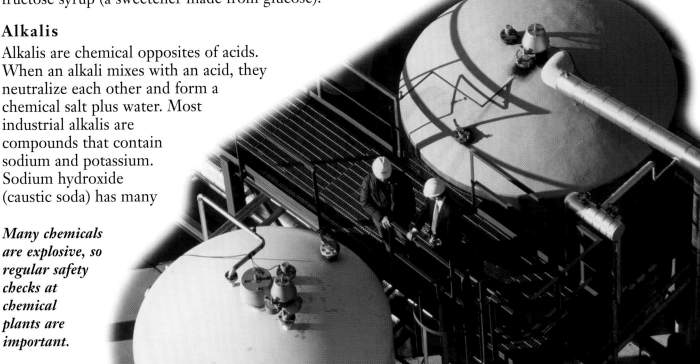

Many chemicals are explosive, so regular safety checks at chemical plants are important.

Civil Engineering

The design and construction of bridges, tunnels, and other large structures

The modern world would grind to a halt without highways, railroads, and airports. These constructions and many other projects are the responsibility of civil engineers, people who design and build structures for the public's benefit. Most civil engineering projects are relatively small. Others, such as major ports or dams, new cities, and reclaiming land from the sea, are huge undertakings. Three of the world's greatest civil engineering structures are big enough to be seen from the Moon: the Suez and Panama Canals, and the Great Wall of China.

What civil engineers do

Civil engineers oversee the construction of a project, such as a bridge or highway. The same team may work on the project from its design on a computer screen right through until it opens to the public. If the structure is particularly complex or involves the risk of major damage to the environment, the process may take many years.

Civil engineers work with people such as architects (who design buildings) and other specialized engineers. Acoustic (sound) engineers might be called in to advise on reducing noise from a new highway by building an embankment or planting a line of tall trees alongside it.

One of the world's longest civil engineering projects, the 2,150-mile (3,460 km) Great Wall of China.

Projects of the past

Although civil engineering is a modern high-technology profession, some ancient civilizations built huge structures. The Romans undertook civil engineering projects throughout their empire. They built a road system that stretched more than 50,000 miles (80,000 km). The Romans built the first large-scale road system including tunnels, developed water-carrying bridges, called aqueducts (AK-wuh-duktz), and constructed many ambitious public buildings, such as the Coliseum. They also built Hadrian's Wall, stretching across northern England.

Modern civil engineering began with military projects in the 18th century. Engineers helped armies build roads and bridges, making it easier

HIGHLIGHTS

- ◆ Civil engineers build major structures such as bridges, highways, and tunnels.

- ◆ Civil engineering involves striking a balance between improving life for people and protecting the environment.

- ◆ Environmental engineers are specialized civil engineers who may be called on to solve environmental problems.

to move artillery and troops quickly from place to place. In 1747, the world's first engineering college was founded in Paris, France. Soon afterward, a number of English engineers began work on major public engineering projects. They included Thomas Telford (1757–1834), who built roads and bridges; James Brindley (1724–1792), who constructed canals, and John Smeaton (1724–1792), who built lighthouses. Smeaton was the first person to call himself a civil engineer.

The most famous of these English engineers was Isambard Kingdom Brunel (1806–1859), who built a number of railroads, bridges, and large ships.

The transportation revolution

The networks of canals, railroads, and highways constructed by these 18th- and 19th-century civil engineers allowed raw materials and finished goods to be moved around quickly. This transportation network played a crucial role in

A "cloverleaf" interchange allows access between two highways.

the Industrial Revolution.

Civil engineers played a part in the development of many methods of transportation. For example, the ever-increasing size of ships led to a need for bigger and deeper ports. The world's largest port, at Rotterdam in the Netherlands, covers 38 square miles (98 sq km). As well as the harbor, engineers built huge defenses to protect the port from the sea, warehouses in which goods are stored, and docks where ships are repaired and upgraded.

With the growth in air traffic since the 1950s, engineers have helped construct many new airports and the transportation systems that link airports with cities. Completed in 1998, Hong Kong International Airport was one of the world's largest construction projects. It cost $1.1 billion and involved moving a volume of earth that was equal to 326 times the size of the Empire State Building.

LOOK CLOSER

Coastal engineering

More than 70 percent of Earth's surface is covered by water, most of it ocean. Where the ocean meets the land, erosion (wearing away) takes place. As waves crash repeatedly against cliffs, the land gradually tumbles into the ocean and is washed away. Beaches too can disappear slowly as waves wash them along the coast in a process called longshore drift.

Civil engineers are often called on to try to limit the effects of coastal erosion. Piles of huge boulders, called breakwaters, are sometimes placed offshore to

protect towns by the sea. The boulders reduce the energy of incoming waves so they do less damage. The U.S. Army Engineering Corps constantly renews beaches in places such as New Jersey, where heavy storms can wash all the sand away overnight.

In 1932, Dutch engineers built a 19-mile (31 km) seawall across the entrance to a sea inlet called the Zuider Zee. Behind this barrier other walls, called dikes, enclose land that has since been reclaimed from the sea. This fertile reclaimed land, termed polders, now forms the Dutch province of Flevoland.

Isambard Kingdom Brunel

During the 19th century, Englishman Isambard Kingdom Brunel (1806–1859) built bridges, ships, and railroads on a grand scale in places in England, Wales, and Ireland. Most of his projects used iron, a material that became widely available as a result of the Industrial Revolution.

Brunel started to make his mark when he was a young man. At the age of 19, he helped his father build a tunnel under the Thames River, in London. Soon afterward, he used iron to construct the magnificent Clifton suspension bridge, which spans the Avon Gorge in Bristol, western England. He was appointed engineer on Britain's Great Western Railway when he was only 27. In that post, Brunel built bridges, tunnels, and many miles of railroad to link London with the west of England.

A few years later, Brunel constructed huge iron ships to carry passengers and freight. The *Great Britain,* built in 1845, was the world's largest vessel at the time, and it was followed by an even larger ship, the *Great Eastern*, in 1858.

Other jobs for civil engineers

Civil engineers often specialize in one kind of project. Some are energy-production specialists. They might be called on to build power plants, oil or gas wells, or hydroelectric dams (which generate electricity from the energy of a rushing river). Projects such as these can be challenging. For example, a nuclear power plant must be constructed from tough materials that will protect the public from radiation if a major accident should occur. An oil rig might have to survive destructive waves in a harsh environment such as the North Sea (the oil-rich area that lies between Britain and Scandinavia).

In many countries, one of the most important jobs for civil engineers is the construction of water-supply and sewage-disposal systems. Even small-scale water projects, such as a new well, can help prevent diseases and save lives.

Civil engineers are often called on to solve environmental problems, such as building coastal defenses to stop the sea from eroding cliffs or beaches. Projects such as these are sometimes known as environmental engineering. Engineers may repair damage to the environment caused by earlier engineering failures or help restore rivers that have been damaged by mining activities, for example. Similarly, civil engineers were called in to make safe the nuclear power plant at Chernobyl, Ukraine, in 1986, after a dangerous explosion. The engineers completely encased the nuclear reactor that been wrecked inside a concrete "coffin" to prevent more radioactive material from escaping.

Civil engineering projects can sometimes be harmful to the environment. Highways may destroy important wilderness areas or wildlife habitats, while dams may flood whole towns and villages, causing thousands of people to lose their homes. When major engineering projects are planned, people who wish to build them often debate with environmental groups about whether the benefits a project will bring are worth the damage it will cause.

Reducing damage

Major civil engineering projects cause harm to the environment. The challenge is to reduce these effects to a minimum. Civil engineers study carefully the possible effects of a new project before it is built. Such a study is known as an environmental impact assessment (EIA). An EIA also looks at alternatives to the project.

Sometimes, engineering projects are believed to be so important that they must go ahead, no matter what effect they have on the environment. In these cases, environmental engineers are usually called on to reduce the damage. For example, if a massive highway is built across an untouched river, reed beds can be planted near the crossing. The reeds help soak up pollutants that leak from the road, such as toxic particles in automobile exhaust fumes. If trees have to be felled along the route of the new highway, others may be planted nearby to replace them. However, stands of small new trees create a different environment from an ancient forest. There is still an environmental loss.

If a new highway cuts through the habitat of endangered species, wildlife experts might be brought in beforehand to round up the animals and release them elsewhere in a safer location. Occasionally, entire meadows have been dug up and replanted in safe areas. Reducing the effects of a civil engineering project on the environment is known as mitigation.

CHECK THESE OUT!
✔BUILDING TECHNIQUES ✔ENGINEERING
✔RAILROAD CONSTRUCTION ✔ROADS

The Itaipu Dam, between Paraguay and Brazil, is the largest hydroelectric power plant on Earth.

Cleaning Agents

**Soaps and detergents
that get things clean**

*The foam produced by soap helps bring chemicals
called surfactants into contact with dirty skin.*

It is a fact of life that things get dirty. Until
the 20th century, the best way to clean clothes
and dishes was to wash them with soap. Then
scientists developed detergents. These cleaning
agents work in a similar way to soap but they
are more powerful. Soap is still important for
washing the skin, but detergents are better for
shampooing hair, washing clothes and dishes,
and cleaning items such as sinks, floors, and cars.

The active ingredients in soaps and detergents
are chemicals called surfactants. Surfactants allow
soaps and detergents to wash away oils and fats
in dirt that are hard to shift with water alone.
The chemicals create foam and bubbles to help
bring them into close contact with the dirty
surface. The surfactants cling to the particles of
oil and fat and lift them clear of the dirty surface
so water can rinse them away. Surfactants also
help dirty surfaces become wet so the dirt can
be carried away easily.

Soaps

Soap is made by boiling a mixture of animal fat
or vegetable oil in a chemical called an alkali
(AL-kuh-ly), usually sodium hydroxide. Animal
fat, called tallow, comes from cattle or from
sheep. Vegetable oil comes from the fruit of
the oil palm tree, or from rapeseed, soybeans,
coconuts, or sunflower seeds.

Soap itself acts as a surfactant, but soap bars
also contain many other chemicals. These
ingredients improve the color, smell, and feel of
the soap. For example, titanium dioxide colors
soap white. Perfumes give soap a more attractive
smell, salt makes it last longer, and moisturizers
and softeners improve its texture. Preservatives
keep the soap fresh. Antibacterial chemicals
(substances that kill bacteria) are also added.

Although good for cleaning skin, soap has one
main drawback. In many places, water contains
naturally occurring minerals that react with soap.
Such water is called hard water. The minerals
limit the ability of soap to foam (form bubbles),
reducing its cleaning power. These minerals also
combine with the soap to create a scum that
clings to fabrics and other surfaces. Soap gels and
liquid soaps often contain synthetic (artificial)
surfactants instead of soap. Synthetic surfactants
form the basis of detergents.

Detergents

German scientists developed the first synthetic
surfactants during World War I (1914–1918),
when there was a shortage of animal fats for
making soap. Unlike soap, detergents based
on synthetic surfactants dissolve easily in cold
water and clean well in hard water.

HIGHLIGHTS

♦ The active ingredients in cleaning agents
   are called surfactants.

♦ Soaps, detergents, and shampoos work
   by dissolving the oils and fats in dirt.

♦ Most cleaning agents contain additives to make
   them look and smell more attractive.

Dry Cleaning

Some clothes, such as suits, cannot be cleaned with water and laundry detergents. Washing would spoil their shape, make them shrink, or damage the fabric. Clothes like this are dry-cleaned instead. Dry cleaning involves treating clothes with chemicals that dissolve away the dirt and then evaporate (turn into gas). The dissolved dirt is carried away by the gas, leaving the clothes dry and clean.

Laundry powder contains surfactants and a substance called a builder. The builder helps the surfactants work more effectively by softening hard water and dispersing dirt. Laundry powder may also contain a bleach to whiten the clothes and additives such as fragrances, enzymes (EN-zims), and optical brighteners. Enzymes are biological substances that break down stains from food, blood, grass, and other natural materials. Some enzymes break down fats that surfactants cannot remove. These enzymes work while the clothes are drying, so they do not remove the fatty stains completely until the next wash.

Bleaches, such as sodium perborate, work by combining the chemicals in certain types of stains with oxygen, making the stains colorless. Optical brighteners make white clothes appear brighter and cleaner. They absorb invisible ultraviolet light and release it as visible white light.

Liquid laundry detergents contain ingredients similar to those in powders. Many people prefer liquid detergents because they dissolve much more easily in water and do not become lumpy like powders if they become damp.

A dishwashing detergent contains cleaning and foaming agents, preservatives, fragrance, coloring, and antibacterials. The detergent dislodges the food particles from the dishes and holds them suspended in the water. The suds produced by the detergent are a good guide to its cleaning power. When all the suds are gone, the detergent has all been used up. Automatic dishwasher detergents produce few suds because they could interfere with the washing action of the machine.

Shampoos and other cleaners

The scum left by soap and water makes hair feel stiff and dirty. Shampoos avoid this problem by using synthetic surfactants, such as alkyl ether sulfate, which do not create a scum. The surfactant creates a foam, and other ingredients in the shampoo make the foam long-lasting.

Additives in shampoos improve their appearance and smell, and make the hair look and feel better. Panthenol (pan-THEE-NOL) is a common additive. It helps hold moisture in the hair and adds body and shine. Conditioning shampoos contain silicone (SIH-luh-KON), a chemical that coats the hair and improves both its strength and appearance.

Household cleaners are available in many forms, including liquids, gels, powders, and solids. Most are designed to deal with specific types of dirt and clean different types of surfaces. Household cleaners contain detergents and other ingredients, such as disinfectants to kill germs and abrasives (uh-BRA-sivs; substances used for rubbing) to shift hardened dirt.

CHECK THESE OUT!
✔ABRASIVE ✔ANTISEPTICS ✔POLLUTION

Discarded detergents can cause pollution in waterways.

Cloning

Producing identical copies of animals, plants, or other organisms from cells of those organisms

Cloning is the production of new, identical organisms (living things) using cells from a single individual. This process takes place naturally in bacteria, plants, and some animals such as aphids. Only recently have scientists succeeded in cloning animals artificially. A clone is identical to its parent in its genetic makeup, that is, it has the same genes. Genes are the parts of cells that control the way a living thing develops. They are located within the nucleus (control center) of each cell and made of DNA.

Scientists do not only clone entire organisms. Cloning also refers to the process of making copies of DNA molecules artificially, or growing identical animal cells to carry out research.

Cloning in the natural world

Many plants and animals clone naturally in a process called asexual reproduction. Females of these organisms produce young identical to

The famous Dolly the sheep. She has no father—all of her genetic information was provided by one of her mother's udder cells.

HIGHLIGHTS

◆ Cloning is the production of identical organisms or DNA molecules from a single cell or tiny sample.

◆ Cloning happens in mammals when twins are born, and in some plants, insects, and microorganisms.

◆ Scientists successfully cloned an adult mammal in 1997. Dolly the sheep was cloned from cells taken from the udder of an adult sheep.

themselves without mating. However, most animals, including all birds and mammals, must mate to reproduce. This sexual reproduction involves the fertilization of a female's eggs by sperm from a male. Both the male and the female contribute genes to the resulting offspring. The fertilized egg cell splits into two and continues to divide to form a bundle of cells that develops into an embryo (unborn young animal). In mammals, cloning occurs naturally when identical twins develop. After the fertilized egg has divided a few times, the cluster of cells separates into two. The cell bundles develop into two offspring with identical genes—they are clones of each other but not of their parents.

Artificial cloning

Many plants can be cloned by rooting a cutting in soil. Some plants are cloned by taking a few cells and growing them in a nourishing gel. This practice is now widespread, although many plants are difficult to grow this way. In animals, the process is even more difficult, despite the fact that the nucleus of each cell contains all the genes needed to make a new individual.

Cloning animals is complicated because of the way that genes behave. As an embryo develops inside its mother, different genes are switched on or off inside each cell, directing its development. Once the genes in animal cells are switched on, it is hard to turn them off again. Also, many cells in the body do not divide once they have specialized into a particular body cell, such as an eye, skin, or heart cell. One cloning technique uses cells from very young embryos that consist of only 32 cells. At this stage of development, the cells have yet to specialize. If the cells are separated and cultured (grown in nutrient liquid), each may grow into a separate individual. This process mimics the way identical twins develop.

Dolly the sheep

In 1997, the Roslin Institute near Edinburgh, Scotland, made an exciting announcement. It reported that a research team had cloned a sheep from a cell taken from the udder of an adult sheep. The cloned sheep, called Dolly, was the first animal to be cloned from a fully developed cell. The news was important because it was clear that the same technique might eventually be used to clone people.

The Roslin team cultured udder cells in a liquid that did not contain enough nutrients. These "starved" cells reset their genes to an embryonic form that allowed cloning to occur. A total of 276 attempts at this process had failed before one was successful. The success was Dolly.

INTO THE FUTURE

A breakthrough in human cloning

In 2001, a U.S. research team, led by Argentine-born Jose Cibelli, successfully cloned several human embryos. The embryos only reached a very early stage of development. The cells divided a few times and the embryos consisted of no more than six cells.

Perhaps the most remarkable aspect of the research was not the cloning, but the success of another experiment carried out at Advanced Cell Technology (ACT), the Massachusetts company behind the work. Chemical "triggers" were used to make unfertilized human egg cells begin to divide and form embryos. This process—called parthenogenesis—is common in insects but is unknown in mammals outside the laboratory. In the future, this procedure could allow scientists to take egg cells from a patient with heart disease, clone them into heart tissue, and patch them back into the patient's heart.

Since Dolly, cloning research has been successful with around 12 other species of mammals. The technique pioneered by the Roslin team will help animal breeders improve their stock much more quickly than through conventional breeding techniques. Animals such as prize cows could be cloned to produce identical copies rather than relying on traditional breeding methods.

CHECK THESE OUT!
✔BIOTECHNOLOGY ✔GENETIC ENGINEERING
✔HORTICULTURE ✔LIVESTOCK FARMING

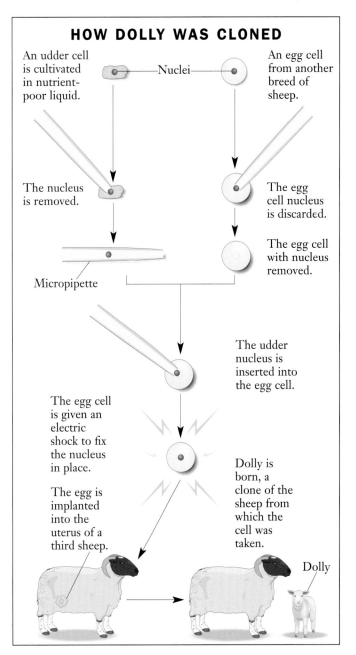

HOW DOLLY WAS CLONED

An udder cell is cultivated in nutrient-poor liquid.

Nuclei

An egg cell from another breed of sheep.

The nucleus is removed.

The egg cell nucleus is discarded.

Micropipette

The egg cell with nucleus removed.

The udder nucleus is inserted into the egg cell.

The egg cell is given an electric shock to fix the nucleus in place.

The egg is implanted into the uterus of a third sheep.

Dolly is born, a clone of the sheep from which the cell was taken.

Dolly

Clothing Industry

**How clothes are designed,
cut, and assembled**

Clothing makers need to design clothes quickly to keep up with changing fashions. They must also make them cheaply and get them into the stores before fashion moves on. Modern technology helps minimize both costs and manufacturing time.

Designing clothes

The first stage in clothing manufacture is design. The designer creates the look and color of the garment, chooses the fabrics, and decides what sorts of buttons and zippers to use.

Instead of drawing on paper, most designers now use computer-aided design (CAD) to sketch out a design. CAD systems enable designers to draw their ideas on computer screens. On screen, a designer can view the garment from various angles and in different patterns and colors. The designer can also change the design, for instance, to find out how the garment would look in leather instead of cotton, or with a narrower waist. CAD systems make the design process quicker and cheaper, and the designer can create many different versions without making a single garment.

The designer eventually has a sample garment made up. A series of basic patterns called slopers are created. One sloper is made for each component (part) of the garment, such as the front, back, and collar, and one for each sleeve and pocket. Using the slopers, the clothing manufacturer makes a sample garment. A model tries on the sample to check its size and to make sure it is comfortable to wear. Only about one new design in four is selected for manufacture as a garment.

The model will have the body size and shape of an ideal customer, but clothes are made in many sizes to fit a wide range of people. The original sample garment is made in a chosen size, called the base size. Patterns for garments in other sizes are made from the base size pattern using a system known as grading. The original pattern is scaled up or down to fit larger or smaller people. Using a CAD system, an operator is able to calculate the sizes of the slopers that are needed to make larger and smaller sizes of the garment.

A designer creates a new garment.

In the next stage of the process, a pattern called a marker is created. A marker is like a jigsaw puzzle, made of all the slopers for a particular size of garment. The slopers fit closely together to form the marker, which is carefully designed so that the cloth can be cut with the minimum of waste. Next, a series of printouts of the marker are used to guide cloth cutters as they cut the components of the garment from a long roll of cloth. CAD is increasingly used at this stage to minimize the amount of waste fabric.

Cutting the cloth

Cloth arrives at the factory in large rolls. In the cutting room, operators or computerized machines unroll the cloth onto long tables. The fabric is either spread out by hand or by a computerized spreading machine. At this stage, operators examine the cloth carefully for defects. The fabric must be laid out flat and with minimum tension. A misshaped piece would be cut if there were any folds or tension in the cloth. That would distort the shape of the final garment. Several layers of cloth, called plies, are placed on top of each other so that they can all be cut at the same time. Then the operators put the marker on the top layer of cloth.

The marker must be held firmly in place or the pieces could be cut inaccurately. It is secured by staples, pins, adhesive, suction, or weights. Cutting by hand, the operators guide their knives, driven by electric motors, through the marker and the layers of the fabric. They follow the lines on the marker to cut out the garment components.

Computerized cutting machines have the marker data programmed into them. The machines use this data to guide their cutting knives automatically. Laser cutting machines work in much the same way, but they cut the cloth using beams of laser light instead of knives.

Other types of cutting machines use jets of high-pressure water or plasma (superheated gas) instead of knives to slice through leather or plastic. These machines can cut at speeds of up to 490 feet (150 m) a minute.

LOOK CLOSER

How Sewing Machines Work

Most sewing machines, both home and industrial, work in the same way. The operator puts the pieces of fabric to be sewn together beneath a presser foot (a footlike metal plate). The foot holds them firmly. An electric motor turns a rotating mechanism called a cam. The cam drives a strong needle up and down through the pieces of fabric. Thread from a spool on the top of the machine passes through a hole in the needle. As the needle moves up and down, it catches a second thread. This thread comes from a second spool (the bobbin), which is mounted below the presser foot. The needle pulls this thread up through the fabric. This process, repeated again and again, interlocks the two threads to stitch the two layers of fabric together.

As well as powering the needle, the electric motor drives a device called a feed dog beneath the presser foot. This device has serrated metal teeth that force the material through the sewing machine. The feed dog ensures that the fabric passes through the machine at the same rate as the needle makes stitches.

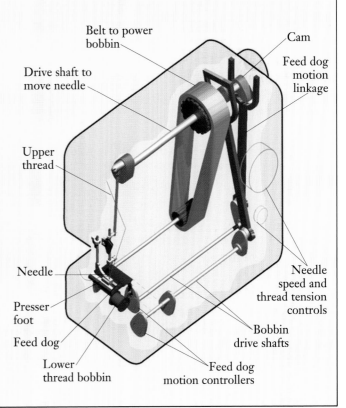

Belt to power bobbin

Cam

Feed dog motion linkage

Drive shaft to move needle

Upper thread

Needle

Presser foot

Feed dog

Lower thread bobbin

Needle speed and thread tension controls

Bobbin drive shafts

Feed dog motion controllers

Assembling the garments

Operators assemble the parts into garments in a sewing room. In the bundle system, one operator gets a bundle of sleeve parts to assemble into sleeves, another gets a bundle of fronts and backs to join together, and so on. Other operators take the completed sleeves and other components and assemble them into complete garments.

The bundle system needs lots of operators and equipment, so some clothing factories use the more economical unit production system instead. All the parts for a single garment are put on an overhead hanger that carries them from one operator to the next. Each operator does one part of the work needed to assemble the garment. A more efficient way to put garments together is to use a system called modular manufacturing. In this system, operators work in groups of 3 to 12. The work benches are arranged in a horseshoe shape, and each operator stitches together an entire garment. The operators move to separate work benches for each stage of the sewing.

The modular system is healthier for the operators, because they perform many different movements while working. In the bundle system and the unit system, they have to make the same movements over and over again, causing muscular and joint problems. The manufacturer also benefits since the system is cheaper because there is a smaller amount of unfinished work in progress at any one time.

Sewing machines

Operators in a sewing room mostly use sewing machines to assemble the garments. Sewing machines are a highly automated version of the traditional needle-and-thread method of sewing by hand. Most sewing machines, both in the home and in the factory, work in the same way. Although home sewing machines can sew many different types of stitches, most types of industrial machines specialize in just one type. Industrial machines are also heavier and stronger and work much faster.

An industrial machine can make more than 6,000 stitches per minute. This is around five times faster than most home machines.

The finishing touches to the garments are usually carried out by machines. These processes include creating the buttonholes and sewing on buttons and zippers. Finally, automatic and semi-automatic pressing machines remove any creases in the fabric, and the garment is ready to leave the factory. Sometimes, garments are manufactured in a neutral color and are dyed later. The color chosen will depend on the demand for particular colors of clothes from the stores.

Automated clothing manufacture produces large numbers of identical garments cheaply. High-fashion items are made in small numbers by much more labor-intensive methods. Some luxury clothing items, such as suits and jackets, are almost entirely handmade.

CHECK THESE OUT!
✔COMPUTER ✔FIBERS AND YARNS ✔FOOTWEAR MANUFACTURE ✔TEXTILES

Clothing manufacture often involves a number of operators working together on a production line.

Coal

A carbon-rich fuel and a source of important chemicals

A mechanical cutter rips coal from an underground seam and drops it onto a conveyor belt.

Fossil fuels consist of the remains of ancient plants and other organisms. Coal, the most plentiful fossil fuel, began to form when dead trees and other plants sank to the bottom of ancient swamps. The plants that form most modern-day coal died during the Carboniferous period, around 300 million years ago.

How dead plants turn into coal

Beneath the mud and stagnant water of swamps, buried plants decay to become peat. Peat is a soft, dark-brown material that can be burned as a fuel. In the depths of peat bogs, the decomposing material reaches temperatures of more than 212°F (100°C). Chemical reactions driven by this heat gradually transform the peat into coal.

As water, carbon dioxide, and methane gas escape from the peat, it slowly becomes a soft, brown coal called lignite. Over millions of years, the lignite changes further, into sub-bituminous and bituminous (buh-TOO-muh-nuhs) coals. These coals are harder than lignite and burn more easily, giving off more heat.

With further compression, these coals turn into anthracite (AN-thruh-SYT). Anthracite is the hardest coal and contains the highest proportion of carbon. When it burns, anthracite produces more heat than the other forms of coal and leaves less ash behind.

Vast reserves

Coal mining began thousands of years ago, but there are still at least 600 billion tons (545 metric tons) left underground. This total is more than 20 times larger than the world's known reserves of oil and natural gas. Most of this coal is in the United States, China, and Eastern Europe. The United States has one quarter of the world's known coal reserves.

The areas where coal is found are called coalfields. Where the coal is close to the surface of the ground, coal miners use bulldozers and other machinery to scrape away the soil and rock that covers it. Then they dig out the exposed coal. This process is called strip mining. Where the coal is deep beneath the ground, miners dig underground shafts and tunnels to get to the seams (layers) of coal. This is called deep mining.

Coal is usually transported by railroad from mines to power stations or distribution centers.

HIGHLIGHTS

◆ Coal is the carbon-rich compressed remains of prehistoric plants.

◆ Coal is burned to produce heat.

◆ Heating coal without burning it produces coal gas, coal tar, and coke.

LOOK CLOSER

Making Coke

Coke producers heat coal but keep air out to stop the coal from burning. This process yields both coal tar and gas, as well as the brittle, porous, carbon-rich solid called coke. The coal is heated in rows of tall, narrow ovens. A single coke-making plant can contain up to 100 ovens. The coke ovens are heated by gas burners in large vertical pipes. Machines remove the red-hot coke when the process is finished. The coke is then cooled in water. Gases given off in the process are recycled. The largest ovens can produce millions of tons of coke a year. Low-temperature heating at 1110° to 1650°F (600° to 900°C) produces a type of coke that is an almost smokeless fuel. When it burns, this coke produces less pollution than coal. Heating coal at higher temperatures, at around 1650° to 2200°F (900° to 1200°C) produces coke with a higher carbon content and fewer impurities. This coke is used in blast furnaces and steelworks.

Coal as a fuel

The Chinese were probably the first people to use coal. Some 3,000 years ago, they burned it to heat furnaces that produced copper and iron. The Romans burned coal for heating and cooking. Deep mining for coal began in Europe in the 13th century. New ways of making iron, and the invention of the steam engine, created an enormous demand for coal during the Industrial Revolution of the 18th century. Steam power throughout the 18th and 19th centuries relied on coal to power ships, railroad locomotives, and electricity generators.

When coal burns, the carbon it contains combines with oxygen in the air to release heat. Gases that cause pollution are also produced. Carbon dioxide and methane are major contributors to global warming. Two other gases, the oxides of sulfur and nitrogen, combine with moisture in the air to form nitric and sulfuric acid. These acids cause acid rain, which

Machinery strips brown coal (lignite) in layers from shallow excavations in Saxony, Germany.

poisons lakes and erodes buildings. Burning coal also releases small amounts of toxic elements into the air. These elements, such as mercury and chlorine, are present in coal as impurities. Other toxic elements, including arsenic and barium, are left behind in the coal ash.

Producing heat for industry

Many industrial plants burn coal to produce heat. They use several methods to make sure the coal burns as completely as possible. The fixed-bed system burns 2-inch (5 cm) lumps of coal on a grate. To make coal burn properly, the system blows one stream of air across the top of the coal and another up through it from below. In the fluidized bed system, a high-speed airstream blows up through crushed coal particles mixed

with sand, ash, or crushed limestone. The air makes the particle mixture bubble like a boiling fluid. Constant movement of coal particles makes them burn efficiently, and the process produces much less pollution than fixed-bed systems.

Power stations burn very small particles of coal to boil water and produce steam. The steam drives turbines that generate electricity. Some power stations burn the coal particles in a stream of air. Others mix the particles with water and burn this mixture like a fuel oil.

Heating without burning

Another way that power stations use coal is by producing coal gas. Coal is heated to around 2900°F (1600°C) without burning it. The heat causes coal gas to be released. This gas is a

mixture of hydrogen, carbon monoxide, and methane. New types of power stations, called IGCC (integrated gasification combined cycle) plants, use coal gas as fuel for gas turbines. They use the hot exhaust gases from the turbines to boil water and make steam for steam turbines. The gas turbines and the steam turbines both drive electricity generators. Until the 1950s, coal gas was the main source of gas for domestic heating and lighting. It was replaced by natural gas, which is cleaner and less toxic to people.

When coal is heated without burning, it also produces a solid residue called coke. Coke is rich in carbon and has many uses in industry. For example, blast furnaces use coke to remove oxygen from iron ore to produce iron.

Chemicals from coal

Coal is an important source of organic (carbon-based) chemicals. These chemicals come from coal tar, another by-product of coal gas production. Early plants that produced coal gas for lighting and heating had no use for the coal tar—they simply dumped the thick, oily liquid. But in the mid-19th century, scientists discovered that coal tar contains a number of important chemicals, such as benzene and toluene. Benzene can dissolve fats and resins, and toluene is an ingredient of some explosives.

Coal tar was soon a major source of organic chemicals. These chemicals became the starting points for a wide range of products, including dyes, perfumes, flavorings, fertilizers, explosives, medicines, and antiseptics. Coal tar is less important today, because most organic chemicals are derived from crude oil.

As the world begins to run out of oil, coal will probably become important as a source of organic chemicals again. Coal might also become the source of oil and gasoline. To make synthetic (artificially produced) oils, oil companies can combine hydrogen with carbon from coal. To make gasoline, they can convert methane gas, which is released by heating coal into methanol. Methanol can then be turned into gasoline.

CHECK THESE OUT!
✔BLAST FURNACE ✔CHEMICAL INDUSTRY
✔IRON AND STEEL ✔MINING ✔POWER STATION

Codes and Ciphers

Methods for keeping information secret

A World War II German Enigma code machine.

Codes and ciphers (SI-fuhrz) are different methods for transforming, or changing, information. Governments, undercover agents, and businesses all use ciphers and codes to protect valuable information. Codes and ciphers are particularly important in times of war.

Letters and languages

A message put into code or cipher is known as a cryptogram (KRIP-tuh-gram). The process of disguising the message is called encryption (in-KRIP-shuhn). Written text, radio and television signals, e-mails, and faxes can all be encrypted using modern technology.

A cipher replaces each letter of an ordinary message with a different letter or symbol, according to a fixed set of rules. A code is more like a secret language. It replaces syllables, groups of letters, or even whole phrases with different symbols according to a prearranged system. In both cases, the person receiving the message must know the key to the system to decipher (understand) the coded message.

Sometimes it is possible for someone else to intercept the message and crack (break) the code. Before the age of computers, codes and ciphers were based on simple rules. Even so, some were

difficult to crack. A famous encryption machine called Enigma was used by German forces during World War II (1939–1945). This allowed 6 trillion possible sequences. This code was eventually broken by the English mathematician Alan Turing (1912–1954).

Since the mid-20th century, computers have revolutionized the process of encryption, which is now much more complex. Now, computer-generated cryptograms are almost impossible for human code-breakers to crack without using powerful computers of their own.

How codes and ciphers work

The simplest way to encrypt a message is to replace each element in it with a different prearranged symbol. This method is called a substitution cipher or code. For example, a letter of the alphabet, such as E, could be replaced by a different letter, say H, each time it occurs. Ciphers that change the order of the letters, or other elements, in a message are called transposition ciphers. Transposition could mean reversing the letters in each word, but keeping the words as distinct units. Some transposition ciphers break the whole message into different units, of four or five letters for example, and are much more difficult to crack.

CHECK THESE OUT!
✔COMMUNICATION NETWORK ✔COMPUTER
✔INFORMATION THEORY ✔TELECOMMUNICATIONS

HIGHLIGHTS

◆ Codes and ciphers are methods of transforming information to make it secret.

◆ The development of computers has revolutionized encryption (code- or cipher-making).

◆ Codes and ciphers generated by modern computers are almost impossible to crack.

Cog Railroad

A railroad designed to transport passengers and cargo up steep slopes

Ordinary railroads cannot climb the steep slopes in mountainous regions. Several types of railroads can tackle these slopes, though. In the 19th and early 20th centuries, these cog, or rack, railroads and various types of cable-operated railroads became the most practical transportation in some mountainous areas. Mountain railroads are also popular tourist attractions in many parts of the world.

How cog railroads work

A cogged (toothed) rail, laid between the ordinary rails, allows the locomotives of cog railroads to climb steep slopes. Toothed gear wheels, or pinions, on the train engage with (grip) the cogged rail, called the rack. The train hauls itself along by gripping the rack with the pinion. In an emergency, the pinion also acts as a brake. Along with the train's regular and emergency brake systems, it helps prevent the train from hurtling back down the slope.

The first cog railroad was built by U.S. engineer Sylvester Marsh (1803–1884) on Mount Washington, New Hampshire, in 1869. Marsh's design was soon in use all around the world, particularly in the Alpine mountain region

in western and central Europe. In 1889, for example, the Pilatus railroad opened in Switzerland, hauling vehicles up gradients of up to 48 percent. This rack railroad is still in use.

Power for cog railways

In the 19th century, the first cog railroads were powered by steam engines. Following the invention of the diesel engine in 1896 by German engineer Rudolf Diesel (1858–1913), diesel engines gradually replaced steam power. Diesel engines provide a smoother driving force than steam-driven locomotives and cause less damage to the rail track.

Today, most cog railroads are powered by electricity, a relatively cheap and reliable form of power. An additional rail may be used to carry the electricity that powers the train, or electricity may be supplied to the motor via a pantograph, or pickup, on top of the locomotive.

Most cog and cable railroads have a single track with a loop where the railcars can easily pass.

Cable-operated railroads

Cable-operated railroads are used on slopes that are so steep not even cog railroads can climb them. The cables, often made from reinforced steel, are set either between or below the tracks to haul railed vehicles up very steep slopes. The railroad carriages start and stop by gripping and releasing the moving cable.

Cable-operated transportation was first developed in the 18th century in mines and quarries to transport heavy loads of coal and other minerals to the surface. Cables attached to coal wagons on tracks were wound around a cable drum. This rotated to winch the wagon upward to the surface. At first, steam power was used to drive the cable drum. The steam engine was housed in a building situated at the surface.

The first cable-operated railroad in everyday use was built in San Francisco in 1873. The system was soon widely used around the world, but improvements in other forms of transportation made the popularity of these cable-operated railroad systems short-lived.

Railroads in which railcars are hauled up slopes by cables, rather than under their own power, are called cable cars, incline railroads (usually shortened to inclines), or (in Europe) funiculars (fyoo-NI-kyuh-lurz).

In cable car or incline systems, two railcars are linked to opposite ends of a long cable. When the system is not operating, one railcar is situated

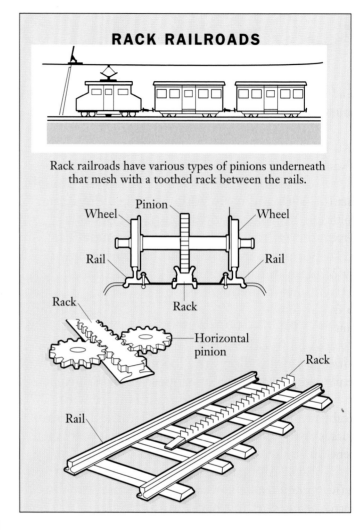

RACK RAILROADS

Rack railroads have various types of pinions underneath that mesh with a toothed rack between the rails.

Wheel — Pinion — Wheel
Rail — Rail
Rack — Rack
Horizontal pinion
Rack
Rail

at the base of the slope and the other is at the top. The cable is usually looped around and powered by a pulley system at the top of the slope. The two cars balance one another as they climb and descend, so relatively little power is needed to run the system.

Cable cars are popular tourist attractions in mountainous regions where they take skiers to the summits. Some cable cars are still used by commuters in hilly cities. Pittsburgh once had 15 of these incline railroads, the first of which was constructed in 1870. Only two incline railroads remain in Pittsburgh. San Francisco is famous for its cable cars, and the historic Angel's Flight incline, in Los Angeles, was restored in 1996 after being dismantled in 1969.

CHECK THESE OUT!
✔BRAKE SYSTEMS ✔RAILROAD CAR ✔RAILROAD
CONSTRUCTION ✔RAILROAD OPERATION

LOOK CLOSER

Cableways

Cableways consist of cabins or containers that are suspended from, and moved on, overhead cables. The cables wind around rotating cable drums that operate in a similar way to cable cars.

Cableways are used in industry and mining. The longest cableway stretches for 60 miles (96 km) in Sweden. Used to transport iron ore until 1987, this cableway now carries tourists. Cabins on cableways take winter sports enthusiasts and other visitors up mountains in many countries. Ski lifts are simplified cableways in which cabins are replaced by individual seats that are suspended from cables.